healthy recipes

healthy
dinner party recipes

Vincent Square Books

This edition published in 2004 by Vincent Square
Books, 3 Vincent Square, London SW1P 2LX

First published in 2003

ISBN 1 85626 597 8

Text © see page 176
Photographs © see page 176

The following are hereby identified as the authors of
this work in accordance with Section 77 of the
Copyright, Designs and Patents Act 1988: Darina
Allen, Hugo Arnold, Aliza Baron Cohen, Ed Baines,
Vatcharin Bhumichitr, Conrad Gallagher, Paul
Gayler, Elisabeth Luard, Adrian Mercuri, Alison
Price, Michael van Straten, Louisa J Walters, Mandy
Wagstaff and Sarah Woodward.

A Cataloguing in Publication record for this title is
available from the British Library.

Printed and bound in China by C & C Offset
Printing Co., Ltd.

contents

introduction

Today's entertaining focuses on providing simple, fresh food to nourish our friends and family. We no longer feel the need to spend hours on end slaving over a hot stove to impress our friends with the latest in food fashions. Eating should be a pleasure, not a competitive sport.

Dinner parties don't need to be an excuse for a complete blow-out either. Many people these days are more health- and weight-conscious, and the recipes in this book demonstrate that you can serve fresh and healthy food to your friends and family without breaking the basics of healthy eating. Nutritional information is given for each recipe so you can easily mix and match to put together a healthy menu.

Many of the recipes in this book are quick and easy to prepare and are perfect for weeknight entertaining when time may be short. Others take longer to prepare and are best reserved for occasions when you have a little more time. Recipes that require marinating can either be prepared in the morning before setting off for work, or made up the night before and left in the fridge for 24 hours. In the evening all you will have to do is fish it out of the marinade and cook it. Desserts such as sorbets can be made several days in advance and kept in the freezer.

The secret of stress-free entertaining is planning. If you haven't got a lot of experience in the kitchen, keep it simple and don't attempt to cook anything too complicated, or something you've not cooked before. Do the shopping the night before, giving you a chance to pick up any ingredients you may not have been able to find on the day itself.

If it's to be a formal occasion, set the table in the morning before you go to work and don't forget to put the wine in the fridge to chill.

Menu-planning is mainly commonsense, but it's better to follow a few principles to avoid potential pitfalls. In general, it's easier to select a main course then choose a starter and dessert to complement. When planning your menu, variety and balance are key. Think of the ingredients, cooking method and colour of the dishes you plan to serve. Don't serve eggs in every course, or three fried dishes, or an all-white plate – think chicken breast, cauliflower and mashed potato – just replacing the cauliflower with carrot will make the food look much more attractive.

Similarly, don't serve three courses that all need be cooked on the night. If you're planning on a stir-fry which needs to be prepared at the last minute, choose a salad as a starter and a sorbet for dessert – that way you'll lower not only your stress levels but also the amount of time you need to spend in the kitchen.

If you get frustrated being in the kitchen while everyone else is enjoying drinks in the next room, choose dishes that need no last-minute preparation, such as a casserole. That way you can prepare everything beforehand and pop it in the oven before your guests arrive, leaving you to give your full attention to your guests. Choose a cold dessert – ice cream or sorbet, for example, and that will cut down even further on the time you need to spend in the kitchen on the night. If on the other hand you do your entertaining in the kitchen you can choose dishes that need last-minute attention and turn the cooking into a communal activity.

tips & shortcuts

dinner party planning

To make sure your dinner party goes without a hitch, it can be a good idea to check if your guests have any dietary restrictions, food allergies or special needs before starting to plan your menu. Peanuts, strawberries and seafood are some of the most common causes of food allergy so avoid these altogether in the whole meal if any of your guests are affected. Vegetarians come in different 'varieties' - check whether your guests eat fish or dairy products before planning the meal. There are plenty of vegetarian and even vegan dishes that even the most ardent of meat-eaters will enjoy. Pork, seafood and alcohol may all pose problems for religious reasons. If in doubt, simply ask your guests.

be creative

If you're planning a barbecue, don't automatically reach for the beefburgers and sausages. Prepared convenience foods tend to be higher in fat and salt than most home-cooked food. Fish and vegetable skewers are quick and easy to prepare and are lower in fat than many traditional barbecue foods. Complement with a couple of salads and some baked potatoes for a balanced meal.

nibbles

If you're serving nibbles before dinner, replace the usual peanuts and crisps with some crudités and a low-fat fromage frais dip. Batons of carrots and cucumber, slices of pepper, cherry tomatoes and florets of cauliflower look attractive arranged on a large plate and won't pile on the calories.

how to use this book

Each recipe provides information about the number of servings it provides, and how long it takes to prepare and cook. As a general principle, the preparation time is the time it takes to wash, prepare and chop the ingredients for the recipe, and the cooking time is the time you actually need to spend cooking, although for much of this time the dish may be able to be left to its own devices while you get on with something else.

In addition, each recipe provides nutritional information. As a rough guide, children, sedentary women and older adults need approximately 1,600 calories per day. Teenage girls, active women and sedentary men need 2,200 calories, and teenage boys, active men and very active women need up to 2,800 per day. Current advice is that no more than 10-30 per cent of our daily energy intake should come from fats. Most of us should be trying to cut down on total fats, and particularly saturated fats.

Carbohydrates are an important part of everyone's diet. It is recommended that at least a third of our daily intake is made up of starchy foods such as potatoes, yams, wholegrain bread, pasta, noodles, chapattis, rice, sweet potatoes and so on.

It is recommended that our daily salt intake not exceed 6g. Most of us consume more like 9g (the equivalent of 2 teaspoonfuls). Much of the salt we consume comes from processed convenience foods, but approximately 10 per cent of it comes from salt we add to our food, either during cooking or at the table. High salt consumption is implicated in raised blood pressure, which is turn has been linked to a higher risk of heart disease and stroke. There is evidence that the fibre contained in wholegrain foods and in fruit and vegetables may protect against developing some forms of heart disease and cancer.

simple
starters
&
suppers

roasted **beetroot** & orange 'latte'

450g (1lb) fresh small beetroots, trimmed
and peeled
1 tablespoon shelled pistachio nuts
grated rind and juice of 4 oranges
75ml (3fl oz) milk
1 small wedge honeydew melon, deseeded

Preheat the oven to 190°C/375°F/gas mark 5. Wrap the beetroot in a loose pouch of foil, sealing the top tightly. Place on a roasting tin and roast for 30-40 minutes until completely tender.

Heat a small frying pan. Add the pistachio nuts and cook for a couple of minutes until toasted and lightly brown, shaking the pan occasionally to prevent them from burning.

Remove the beetroots from the oven and tip the contents of the foil pouch into a food processor or liquidiser. Blend to a purée, then with the machine still running, slowly pour in the orange juice and add half of the rind. Finally, pour in two thirds of the milk until just combined.

Switch off the machine and season to taste. Pour into heatproof glasses and sprinkle the toasted pistachios on top. Steam the remaining milk using a cappuccino steamer or whisk and then carefully spoon on top of the beetroot mixture. Sprinkle over the remaining orange rind and pare shavings of the melon on top to serve.

TIP

Having a cappuccino maker helps for this recipe but don't worry if you don't have access to one. There are now a number of decent gadgets available in cookshops which do a perfectly adequate job.

Nutritional value per serving:

Calories: 96

Fats: 2g

Carbohydrates: 17g

Salt: 0.25g

Saturated fat: 0.4g

Fibre: 2.4g

oyster salad

2 dozen oysters, shucked and roughly chopped

2 yellow or green chillies, deseeded
    and finely chopped

2-3 spring onions, trimmed and roughly chopped

4 tablespoons lime or lemon juice or white
    wine vinegar

salt

To serve
chopped coriander
pickled chillies
quartered limes or lemons

Combine all the ingredients, leave to marinate for 3-4 hours, drain, spoon back into the shells or glass bowls, dress with freshly chopped coriander and serve well chilled, with the pickled chillies and quartered limes.

How to open oysters

Fold up a tea towel and place on the palm of your hand for protection. With the flat side of the oyster uppermost and the pointed end facing towards you, slide the point of an oyster knife between the two shells to sever the nerve holding the oyster closed. Remove the top shell and discard. Slide the knife under the oyster in the shell to cut it loose from the bottom shell. Remove the oyster, or leave in the shell if serving whole.

 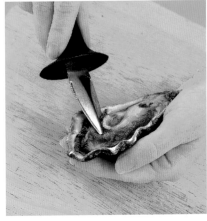

Nutritional value per serving:

Calories: 51

Fats: 1g

Carbohydrates: 2g

Salt: 1.22g

Saturated fat: 0.2g

Fibre: 0.1g

mixed ceviche

225g (8oz) salmon fillets

225g (8oz) John Dory, brill or turbot fillets

225g (8oz) mackerel fillets

juice and zest of 4 limes

juice and zest of 2 lemons

juice of 1 orange

1 tablespoon white wine vinegar

300g (10$\frac{1}{2}$ oz) unpeeled potatoes (preferably a waxy salad variety, like Charlotte, pink fir apple or la ratte), sliced into 5mm ($\frac{1}{4}$ in) thick discs

5 tablespoons extra-virgin olive oil

bunch of chives, finely chopped

4 handfuls of mixed salad leaves

salt and freshly ground pepper

Well ahead, ideally the day before: cut the fish into strips about 2cm ($\frac{3}{4}$in) thick and place in a bowl. Sprinkle with the juice and zest from the limes, lemons and orange, together with the vinegar. Cover and refrigerate for 6 hours, or preferably overnight.

Boil the potatoes in boiling salted water until just tender, drain and refresh in cold water, but try to keep them slightly warm. Pile the potato slices in the centre of 4 plates. Drizzle over a little olive oil and season with salt and pepper. Strain the fish, reserving the citrus juices, and scatter the pieces around the potatoes. Sprinkle over the chives and top with the salad leaves.

Combine a dessertspoon of the reserved citrus juices with 3 tablespoons of olive oil, season with salt and pepper and pour over the salad leaves to serve.

How to skin fish fillets

Put the fillet of fish skin-side down onto a chopping board. With the knife at 45˚ angle, cut through the flesh down onto the skin at the tail end. Hold on to the skin and half push, half saw the flesh off the skin. Use the skins for fish stock.

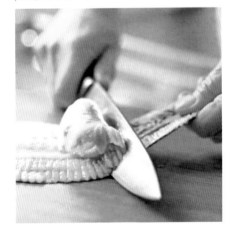

Nutritional value per serving:

Calories: 465

Fats: 30g

Carbohydrates: 15g

Salt: 0.52g

Saturated fat: 5g

Fibre: 1.1g

peruvian **ceviche**

900g (2lb) fillets of monkfish, cod, plaice,
　lemon sole or scallops
4 limes
2 lemons
2 garlic cloves, finely chopped
fresh coriander, chopped
1-2 fresh chillies
75g (3oz) onions, finely sliced
1 green pepper, finely diced
1 red pepper, finely diced
salt and freshly ground black pepper

To serve
crisp lettuce leaves
5-6 spring onions
sweetcorn, optional
2 avocados
diced peppers

Skin the fish; slice or cube into 1cm ($\frac{1}{2}$in) pieces and put into a deep stainless steel or china bowl. Squeeze the juice from the limes and lemons and pour over the fish. Sprinkle with salt, pepper and garlic. Cover and leave to marinate for 2-3 hours in a fridge.

Next add the fresh coriander, onions, chillies and the red and green peppers. Cover and leave for $2\frac{1}{2}$ hours in the fridge. Then serve or keep covered until later.

To serve: arrange a few crisp lettuce leaves on a plate and place a tablespoon of ceviche in the centre. Decorate with slices of avocado, diced peppers, sweetcorn and spring onions. Serve it with crusty white bread or tortillas.

Nutritional value per serving:
Calories: 133
Fats: 6g
Carbohydrates: 5g
Salt: 0.34g
Saturated fat: 0.8g
Fibre: 2g

crab & avocado **towers**

2 Hass avocados, skinned, stone removed and
cut into small dice

juice of 1 lime

450g (1lb) cooked white crabmeat, shell
removed

10 plum tomatoes, skinned, deseeded and cut
into small dice (see below)

2 shallots, finely diced

1/4 tea cup chopped chives

3 tablespoons lemon-flavoured olive oil, or
extra-virgin olive oil

salt and freshly ground black pepper

Dressing

2 tablespoons white wine vinegar

1 teaspoon of caster sugar

4 tablespoons extra-virgin olive oil

2 tablespoons chopped dill

salt and freshly ground black pepper

Mix all the ingredients for the dressing.

Line a flat tray with plastic wrap. To assemble the towers: place 10 ring moulds, 7 x 3cm (2³/₄ x 1¹/₄in) deep, on the tray. Mix the avocado with the lime juice, season and divide into 10 equal amounts. Spoon into the base of each mould and smooth with the back of a teaspoon. Repeat with the white crab meat. Mix the tomatoes, shallot, chives and olive oil, season, then layer as before.

With a palette knife or fish slice, place a tower in the centre of each plate. Remove the moulds carefully. Drizzle the dressing around the plate and serve.

How to skin tomatoes

Cut a cross into the base of each tomato and plunge into a bowl of hot water. Leave for a few minutes until the skins start to wrinkle. The skins will then be easy to peel off.

Nutritional value per serving:

Calories: 194

Fats: 16g

Carbohydrates: 3g

Salt: 0.85g

Saturated fat: 2.1g

Fibre: 1.6g

chilli-pickled orange, feta & olive salad

4 oranges, preferably navel

75ml (3fl oz) white wine vinegar

3 tablespoons caster sugar

1 red chilli, thinly sliced into rings

75ml (3fl oz) olive oil

2 tablespoons black olives, stoned

175g (6oz) feta, cut into 1cm ($\frac{1}{2}$in) cubes

1 tablespoon chopped fresh oregano or parsley

baby spinach and rocket leaves, to garnish
   (optional)

salt and freshly ground black pepper

Peel the oranges, being sure to remove all the white pith, and cut them into slices 5mm ($\frac{1}{4}$in) thick. Remove any pips and put the orange slices in a shallow dish. Boil the vinegar and sugar together for 2-3 minutes, add the chilli and then pour on to the orange slices. Cover and leave overnight.

The next day, drain off the juices from the pickled oranges into a bowl. Whisk in the olive oil to make a dressing and season with salt and pepper. Arrange the oranges in a serving bowl. Stir the olives, feta and oregano or parsley into the dressing and sprinkle it over the oranges. Sprinkle with coarsely cracked black pepper, scatter over the spinach and rocket leaves, if using, and serve.

TIP

Haloumi or a firm goat's cheese can be used instead of feta.

Some people like to soak feta cheese in warm water or milk before using. This effectively softens the strong, salty flavour.

Nutritional value per serving:

Calories: 406

Fats: 30g

Carbohydrates: 27g

Salt: 2.23g

Saturated fat: 8.5g

Fibre: 2.1g

SERVES 4

PREPARATION TIME: 10 MINUTES

COOKING TIME: 20 MINUTES

beetroot, tomato & coriander salad with labna

400g (14oz) new-season baby beetroot

200g (7oz) red cherry tomatoes, halved

100g (3^1/$_2$ oz) yellow cherry tomatoes, halved

juice of ^{1}/$_2$ lemon

6 tablespoons virgin olive oil

^{1}/$_2$ teaspoon coriander seeds, lightly cracked in
    a pestle and mortar

cayenne pepper

100g (3^1/$_2$ oz) fresh coriander, leaves only

20 small balls of labna cheese

Place the beetroot in a pan, cover with cold water and bring to the boil. Reduce the heat to a simmer and cook until they are just tender (alternatively, you could steam them). Drain well and peel. Cut the beetroot into halves or quarters, so they are approximately the same size as the tomatoes. Place the beetroot and tomatoes in a large bowl and add the lemon juice, olive oil and coriander seeds. Season with salt and a little cayenne and toss the whole lot together. Finally toss in the fresh coriander leaves, then serve, topped with the balls of labna cheese.

TIP

Labna is a strained yogurt cheese, available from Middle Eastern food shops and some supermarkets. It is easy to make at home: simply strain some thick, Greek-style yogurt through a piece of muslin over a period of two days to drain off the whey, leaving you with a firm yogurt cheese. Roll into small balls between your hands.

Nutritional value per serving:

Calories: 2.54

Fats: 19g

Carbohydrates: 12g

Salt: 0.94g

Saturated fat: 3.6g

Fibre: 2.7g

rice paper wraps with a spicy **soy** dip

150g (5oz) sushi-quality tuna (ie extremely
   fresh), the tail end
50g (2oz) mangetout, cut into thin matchsticks
50g (2oz) carrot, cut into thin matchsticks
50g (2oz) daikon radish, cut into thin
   matchsticks
1 punnet of mustard and cress, cut from base
1 tablespoon sweet soy sauce
juice and zest of 2 limes
1 tablespoon sushi vinegar
8 sheets of rice paper, 21cm (8$\frac{1}{2}$in) round
black sesame seeds for garnish

Spicy soy dip
2 tablespoons light soy sauce
1 tablespoon sugar
1 tablespoon sushi vinegar
1 teaspoon ginger, peeled and finely chopped
1 garlic clove, finely chopped
2 teaspoons sweet chilli sauce
salt and freshly ground black pepper

Nutritional value per wrap:
Calories: 15
Fats: 0g
Carbohydrates: 2g
Salt: 0.34g
Saturated fat: 0.1g
Fibre: 0.1 g

First prepare all the ingredients. Line a tray with parchment paper. Slice the tuna into wafer-thin discs and set aside. On a separate tray, lay out the vegetables and cress. For the marinade, combine the sweet soy sauce, zest and juice of limes, and sushi vinegar in a bowl. Mix together all the ingredients for the spiced soy dip.

Soak the rice paper in a bowl of cold water for 3-4 minutes until soft. Remove from the water and cut on the diagonal into triangle quarters, laying these on a tea towel so that all the points are facing the same way; season. Dip the tuna in the marinade and place on the rice-paper triangles at the opposite side to the points. Place 3 pieces of each vegetable on the tuna and top with cress. Roll up the rice paper, then place each wrap on a tray lined with a cloth. Cover the wraps with cling film to prevent them drying out. Refrigerate until needed.

To serve, place the wraps on a tray and sprinkle liberally with sesame seeds. Transfer the dip into a small bowl and serve.

TIP
If you do not like tuna, use fresh salmon or cooked tiger prawns instead.

yellow courgette &
prawn couscous

275g (10oz) couscous

500ml (18fl oz) boiling water

2 tablespoons light olive oil

16 large raw prawns, de-veined

1 red chilli, deseeded and finely chopped

1 garlic clove, crushed

4 small yellow courgettes, sliced

2 tablespoons flaked almonds, toasted

25g (1oz) sultanas

12 black olives

2 tablespoons chopped fresh mint

1 teaspoon chopped preserved salted lemon

salt and freshly ground black pepper

Dressing

125ml (4fl oz) olive oil

juice of 1 lemon

1 garlic clove, crushed

1 tablespoon white wine vinegar

1 tablespoon chopped fresh mint

Place the couscous in a large bowl, pour over the boiling water, then cover and leave for 5 minutes. Fluff up the couscous with a fork, then cover again and leave for 5 minutes longer. Fluff up again and season to taste.

Heat the oil in a frying pan, add the prawns, chilli, garlic and courgettes and sauté for 3-4 minutes, until the prawns and courgettes are cooked. Add the toasted almonds, sultanas, olives, mint and preserved lemon, then season to taste. Add to the couscous and toss well together.

Whisk all the ingredients for the dressing together and season to taste. Toss with the couscous and serve warm.

TIP

Chicken or salmon could be used instead of the prawns.

Preserved lemons can be found in Mediterranean delicatessens.

Nutritional value per serving:

Calories: 612

Fats: 39g

Carbohydrates: 42g

Salt: 1.38g

Saturated fat: 5.1g

Fibre: 1.4g

pastrami-style salmon with herb oil

juice of 2 lemons

200ml (7fl oz) olive oil

4 tablespoons chopped mixed herbs (such as
   dill, coriander and chervil)

350g (12oz) salmon fillet (not from the tail end)

1 tablespoon coriander seeds

60g (2^1/$_2$oz) coarse sea salt

grated rind of 1 lemon

2 tablespoons Dijon mustard

50g (2oz) crème fraîche

Place half the lemon juice in a screw-topped jar with the olive oil and three tablespoons of the herbs. Season generously and shake well to combine, then store in the fridge for 2-3 days to allow the flavours to develop.

Preheat the grill. Skin the salmon, then run your fingers against the grain of the flesh and remove the pin bones with tweezers. Place the coriander seeds on a baking tray and toast under the grill for a few minutes. Allow to cool, then crush in a pestle and mortar until coarsely ground. Place the crushed coriander seeds in a bowl and add the salt, lemon rind and a good grinding of black pepper. Lay out a double layer of cling film at least twice the size of the salmon and scatter over half the salt mixture and then sprinkle half of the remaining lemon juice on top. Cover with the salmon and scatter over the remaining salt mixture, finishing with the rest of the lemon juice. Wrap well with the cling film, place on a tray and chill for 24 hours.

Unwrap the salmon, then scrape off and discard the first marinade. Stir the remaining tablespoon of herbs into the mustard. Lay out a fresh piece of cling film and smear the top of the salmon with half of the mustard mixture. Place the smeared side of the salmon down on the cling film and smear the other side using the rest of the mustard mixture. Wrap tightly in the cling film, place on a tray and chill for another 24 hours.

Remove the salmon from the fridge and slice as thinly as possible. Arrange a few slices in the centre of each serving plate. Remove the herb oil from the fridge and shake well to combine, then drizzle a little on to each plate. Dot the crème fraîche around the edges of the plates to serve.

Nutritional value per serving:

Calories: 630

Fats: 60g

Carbohydrates: 3g

Salt: 4.44g

Saturated fat: 10.8g

Fibre: 0.1g

SERVES 4

PREPARATION TIME: 10 MINUTES

COOKING TIME: 20 MINUTES

MARINATING TIME: 1-2 DAYS

hot-pickled mackerel

2 large or 4 small mackerel, gutted and
   beheaded

salt

1 heaped tablespoon of flour

2 tablespoons of olive oil

1/2 onion, skinned and finely sliced

1 garlic clove, skinned and crushed

1 mild green chilli, sliced

1 tablespoon chopped parsley

1 bay leaf, torn

6 peppercorns, roughly crushed

3-4 sprigs thyme

4 tablespoons sherry vinegar (or any other
   good vinegar)

2 tablespoons water

Chop each mackerel straight through the bone to give 4-6 thick steaks (your fishmonger will do this for you). Sprinkle with salt and dust with flour. Heat the oil in a shallow frying pan and when it has a blue haze, put in the fish and fry gently until golden and firm (4-8 minutes depending on thickness). Transfer to a wide shallow dish.

Add the onion, garlic and sliced chilli to the oil remaining in the pan (or a little new oil, if using leftovers) and fry gently for a few moments so that the flavours blend. Add the remaining ingredients and allow the mixture to bubble up. Pour this warm scented bath, unstrained, over the fish. Cover loosely with a clean cloth, and leave overnight, at least, in a cool place. Ready to eat in a day, better in two.

Nutritional value per serving:
Calories: 301
Fats: 22g
Carbohydrates: 7g
Salt: 0.42g
Saturated fat: 3.8g
Fibre: 0.6g

palmheart salad with crab

1 can palmhearts, sliced into fine ribbons

6 tablespoons olive oil

2 tablespoons lime juice

shake of Tabasco sauce

1 teaspoon rough salt

To serve

1 cos lettuce, shredded

about 350g (12oz) crabmeat (save the
  carapace for serving)

shredded fresh coconut

Combine the palmhearts with the dressing ingredients, leave to marinate for an hour or two, toss with the shredded lettuce and crabmeat and finish with finely shredded coconut.

TIP

To prepare canned palmhearts (perfect for the dish), cut off any tough outside pieces and use a potato peeler to cut tagliatelli-like ribbons - also a good technique should you manage to lay your hands on fresh palmhearts.

Nutritional value per serving:

Calories: 297

Fats: 23g

Carbohydrates: 3g

Salt: 2.22g

Saturated fat: 4.1g

Fibre: 1.6g

SERVES 20

PREPARATION TIME: 20 MINUTES

COOKING TIME: 40 MINUTES

manhattan **clam** chowder

unscented vegetable oil

5 medium onions, peeled, cut into large dice

8 garlic cloves, finely chopped

1 head of celery, washed, peeled and diced

110g (4oz) lardons of smoked bacon

4.5kg (10lb) fresh clams, washed and rinsed of
   sand and grit

600ml (1 pint) dry white wine

1.8 litres (3 pints) thick tomato juice

3.6 litres (6 pints) fish stock

2 teaspoons Tabasco sauce

2 bay leaves

5 corn on the cob, cooked and kernels removed

1kg (2lb 4oz) potatoes, diced and cooked

12 plum tomatoes, peeled, deseeded and diced

1 tablespoon caster sugar

salt and freshly ground black pepper

$^1/_2$ tea cup flat-leaf parsley, washed, dried and
   chopped, to garnish

Heat a little oil in a saucepan that is large enough to cook the clams. Add the onion, garlic, celery and bacon, then sauté until soft. Turn up the heat and add the clams and white wine. Cover with a lid and cook for about 4-5 minutes until the clams open. Remove the clams from the shells, discarding any that have not opened; reserve 12 for garnishing and set the rest aside.

Return the pan to the heat with the cooking liquid. Add the tomato juice, fish stock, Tabasco and bay leaves and bring to the boil; simmer for 20 minutes. Season, then add the sweetcorn, potatoes, clams, tomatoes and sugar. Check the seasoning, pour into a bowl, sprinkle with parsley and garnish with the clams in their shells.

Nutritional value per serving:

Calories: 174

Fats: 4g

Carbohydrates: 21g

Salt: 1.69g

Saturated fat: 0.8g

Fibre: 2.8g

scallops with ginger, **spring onion** & tamarind

1 tablespoon tamarind paste

2cm ($^3/_4$in) piece of ginger, peeled and grated

2 spring onions, thinly sliced lengthways and
     soaked in iced water

3 tablespoons vegetable oil, plus more for frying

1 tablespoon toasted sesame oil

12 scallops

salt

Place the tamarind paste in a saucepan with 4 tablespoons of water and heat gently, stirring to extract as much of the tamarind as possible. Set aside and allow to cool.

Strain and combine with the grated ginger, drained spring onions and both types of oil.

Season the scallops with salt. Get a frying pan good and hot and then oil it lightly. When the oil is hot, fry the scallops over as high a heat as you can manage for no more than 45 seconds on each side.

Place the scallops on small shallow plates or, better still, in well-scrubbed scallop shells, and spoon over the tamarind mixture.

TIP

If the scallops are really thick, they will sometimes remain cold and uncooked in the middle in the time it takes the exterior to cook perfectly. You can avoid this – and make the scallops go further – by cutting them across into two rounds.

Nutritional value per serving:

Calories: 214

Fats: 12g

Carbohydrates: 3g

Salt: 0.92g

Saturated fat: 1.7g

Fibre: 0.1g

cellophane **noodle salad** with chicken & shrimps

7g ($^1/_4$oz) Chinese mushrooms (wood ears)

600ml (1 pint) chicken stock

2 skinless chicken breasts

200g (7oz) cellophane noodles

75g (3oz) mooli or French radishes

3 tablespoons *nam pla* (Thai fish sauce)

3 tablespoons lime juice, freshly squeezed

1 scant tablespoon caster sugar

2-4 Thai red chillies, deseeded and finely
    chopped

1 red onion, thinly sliced

2 spring onions, thinly sliced at an angle

a few tender celery leaves (optional)

32 cooked Pacific or Dublin Bay prawns or
    48 smaller shrimps

110g (4oz) coriander leaves

salt and freshly ground pepper

sprigs of coriander and a couple of red and
    green chillies, to garnish

Put the mushrooms into a bowl, cover with warm water and allow to reconstitute for about 15 minutes. Drain, rinse and trim off any hard bits. Slice into thin strips.

Bring the chicken stock to the boil, add salt and slip in the chicken breasts; bring back to the boil and simmer gently for 8 minutes. Remove from the heat, cover and allow to cool. Then shred the chicken.

Put the noodles into another bowl, cover with boiling water and allow to stand for 5 minutes. Drain, cut into 8-10cm (3-4in) lengths with a knife or clean scissors. Peel the mooli or radishes and slice very thinly. Put in a bowl of iced water to crisp up.

Mix the fish sauce, lime juice, sugar and chopped chillies in a large bowl. Add the onions, spring onions, celery leaves and wood ears and mix well.

Drain the mooli well and add with the noodles, shrimps, chicken and coriander to the other ingredients. Toss gently. Taste and correct seasoning. Serve garnished with coriander sprigs and a few slices of red and green chillies.

Nutritional value per serving:

Calories: 206

Fats: 3g

Carbohydrates: 24g

Salt: 1.88g

Saturated fat: 0.4g

Fibre: 1g

steamed sea bass with black bean sauce

1cm (^{1}/$_2$in) piece of ginger, peeled and thinly
   sliced
4 spring onions, halved lengthways
1 sea bass, weighing about 800g (1^3/$_4$lb)
4 heads of pak choi, trimmed
3 tablespoons vegetable oil

Black bean sauce
3 tablespoons fermented black beans, roughly
   chopped
1 tablespoon soy sauce
1 dessertspoon medium dry sherry
1 dessertspoon rice vinegar
pepper

To serve
1 dessertspoon toasted sesame oil
1 dessertspoon sesame seeds, toasted in a dry
   frying pan
1 tablespoon chopped coriander leaves

Make the black bean sauce: combine the black beans, soy sauce, sherry, rice vinegar and a generous seasoning of pepper, together with 2 tablespoons of water. Set aside.

Place the ginger and spring onions inside the fish's cavity. Arrange the stuffed fish and pak choi on a plate in a steamer and cook for 10-15 minutes, or until the fish is just cooked. Transfer the fish and pak choi to a low oven and keep warm. Pour the fish juices into the black bean sauce.

Heat a frying pan and, when hot, add the oil. Seconds later, add the black bean sauce mixture and stir to emulsify, cooking the sauce for about 1 minute. Remove from the heat.

Remove the flesh from the carcass of the fish and serve it on top of the pak choi with a generous scoop of the sauce, a drizzle of sesame seed oil, a sprinkling of toasted sesame seeds and a little fresh coriander.

Nutritional value per serving:
Calories: 265
Fats: 13g
Carbohydrates: 4g
Salt: 1.17g
Saturated fat: 1.7g
Fibre: 0.5g

meatballs in broth with oregano

Meatballs

1 tablespoon rice

350g (12oz) finely minced meat (pork and/or beef)

1 egg, mixed with a fork

1 garlic clove, very finely chopped

$^1/_2$ onion, very finely chopped

1 tablespoon chopped or crumbled oregano

$^1/_2$ teaspoon ground allspice

1 teaspoon finely chopped fresh chilli or $^1/_2$ teaspoon chilli flakes

salt

chopped tomato, to serve

Broth

1.2 litres (2 pints) strong chicken, beef or marrow-bone broth

1-2 habanero or malagueta chillies

1-2 sprigs dried oregano

Put the rice in a small bowl with enough boiling water to cover, and leave to soak and swell for about 20 minutes. Drain the rice and put it in a food processor with the rest of the meatball ingredients. Process all to a paste. With wet hands (keep a bowl of warm water handy for rinsing your fingers), form the mixture into about 24 bite-sized balls.

Bring the broth to the boil with the chilli and oregano (tied into a scrap of muslin for ease of removal). Slip in the meatballs and bring back to a simmer. Put the lid on loosely and leave to cook gently until the meatballs are tender - 20-25 minutes. Serve in bowls, finished with a little chopped tomato.

Nutritional value per serving:

Calories: 203

Fats: 10g

Carbohydrates: 7g

Salt: 1.44g

Saturated fat: 3.6g

Fibre: 0.5g

seared **beef roll** with ginger, carrot & peppers

450g (1lb) thinly sliced piece of sirloin
   steak, trimmed

110g (4oz) fresh root ginger, peeled and cut
   into thin matchsticks

2 large carrots, peeled and cut into thin
   matchsticks

6 jalapeño chillies, deseeded and cut into thin
   matchsticks

2 red or yellow peppers, halved, deseeded and
   cut into thin matchsticks

1 jar of palm hearts, drained and cut into thin
   matchsticks

a little olive oil

Place the sirloin steak on a piece of cling film and cover with another piece. Bat out with a rolling pin until you have achieved a rectangle that is 7.5cm x 10cm (3in x 4in) in total, trimming down any ragged pieces around the edges – these can be used in another dish or for a sauce. Remove and discard the cling film.

Layer the ginger, carrots, jalapeño chillies, peppers and hearts of palm matchsticks on to the middle of the beef, leaving two thirds of the meat uncovered with at least a 1cm ($^{1}/_{2}$in) border at the bottom edge. Roll up the beef around the vegetables, forming a tight tube similar to a sushi roll.

Heat a large frying pan. Add a little olive oil and when the oil is smoking, add the sirloin roll to the pan and sear evenly on all sides. Using a pair of tongs, remove the beef roll from the pan and transfer to a chopping board. Cut in half and then into quarters. Arrange in warmed wide-rimmed bowls and serve with a small dish of teriyaki dipping sauce and some Thai sticky rice, if liked.

TIP

The sirloin steak needs to be a thin slice in one whole piece, otherwise you'll have great difficulty making the recipe work. Alternatively, try securing the roll with cocktail sticks which can be removed before carving.

Nutritional value per serving:

Calories: 264

Fats: 9g

Carbohydrates: 17g

Salt: 0.28g

Saturated fat: 2.5g

Fibre: 4.5g

delicious
dinners

french **onion** soup

50g (2oz) butter

1.3kg (3lb) onions, thinly sliced

1.8 litres (3 pints) good beef, chicken or
   vegetable stock

6 slices French bread (baguette), 1cm ($^1/_2$in)
   thick, toasted

75g (3oz) Gruyère cheese, grated

salt and freshly ground pepper

Melt the butter in a saucepan. Add the onions and cook over a low heat for about 40-60 minutes with the lid off, stirring frequently – the onions should be dark and well caramelised but not burnt. Add the stock, season with salt and freshly ground pepper, bring to the boil and cook for a further 10 minutes. Ladle into deep soup bowls, and put a piece of toasted baguette covered with grated cheese on top of each one. Pop under the grill until the cheese melts and turns golden. Serve immediately but beware – it will be very hot. Bon appetit!

Nutritional value per serving:

Calories: 280

Fats: 12g

Carbohydrates: 34g

Salt: 1.97g

Saturated fat: 7.3g

Fibre: 3.5g

polenta & potato soup

2-3 large potatoes, peeled and chunked

1 thick slice pumpkin, skinned and cut into
   chunks

1.2 litres (2 pints) chicken or beef stock or plain
   water

1 onion, finely chopped

2-3 garlic cloves, finely chopped

4 level tablespoons coarse-milled polenta

1 teaspoon chilli flakes or finely chopped
   fresh chilli

handful fresh basil leaves, stripped from
   the stalks

2 hard-boiled eggs, peeled and quartered

salt

Put the potatoes, pumpkin and stock or water in a roomy pan with the onions and garlic. Bring to the boil, stir in the polenta, add a little salt and bring back to the boil. Put the lid on loosely, turn down the heat and simmer for 30-40 minutes until the polenta is perfectly soft and the vegetables are tender. Finish with chilli flakes, basil and quartered hard-boiled eggs.

Nutritional value per serving:

Calories: 204

Fats: 4g

Carbohydrates: 34g

Salt: 1.37g

Saturated fat: 0.9g

Fibre: 2.9g

jerusalem **artichoke** & mushroom stew

900g (2lb) Jerusalem artichokes

1 lemon

4 tablespoons olive oil

2 large onions, finely chopped

2 garlic cloves, finely chopped

225g (8oz) mushrooms, diced

1 teaspoon dried thyme

1 small wine glass white wine

2 tablespoons green olives, stoned and chopped

handful of chopped coriander

1 slice stale bread, crumbled

1 hard-boiled egg, chopped

salt and freshly ground black pepper

To serve

crumbled white cheese or hard-boiled egg

crisp lettuce leaves for scooping

Peel the artichokes carefully and divide into bite-sized pieces. As you peel each root, drop it into a bowlful of cold water into which you have squeezed a little lemon juice.

Heat the oil in a roomy casserole and fry the chopped onion and garlic until soft and golden (don't let it brown). Push aside and add the mushrooms. As soon as they yield up their juices, add the artichokes and the olives. Let them sizzle for a moment. Stir in the thyme, season with salt and pepper, pour in the wine and same volume of water and let everything bubble up.

Turn down the heat, cover loosely and leave to simmer very gently for an hour until the roots are perfectly tender. Stir in the crumbs - they'll soak up all the aromatic juices, leaving the tubers bathed in a deliciously fragrant dressing. Crumble over cheese or hard-boiled egg and serve with crisp lettuce leaves to scoop up the stew.

Nutritional value per serving:

Calories: 332

Fats: 14g

Carbohydrates: 42g

Salt: 0.72g

Saturated fat: 2.1g

Fibre: 5g

tagliatelle with **roasted chicken leg, mushrooms & chilli**

8 chicken legs (preferably free-range)

2 tablespoons olive oil

400g (14oz) fresh tagliatelle

6 shallots, finely chopped

$^1/_2$ red chilli, seeded and finely chopped

310g (11oz) shiitake mushrooms, sliced

4 tablespoons chopped fresh coriander

Preheat the oven to 180°C/350°F/gas mark 4. Place the chicken legs in a roasting tin and drizzle with a little olive oil. Season and roast for 20-30 minutes, depending on the size of the legs, until just tender and cooked through.

Increase the oven temperature to 200°C/400°F/gas mark 6 and roast the chicken legs for another 10 minutes or until the skin is crisp and golden brown.

Meanwhile, cook the tagliatelle in a large pan of boiling salted water for 2 minutes until al dente. Drain and quickly refresh under cold running water.

Heat the remaining tablespoon of olive oil in a large non-stick frying pan and add the shallots. Cook for 1 minute, stirring, then add the chilli and shiitake mushrooms. Increase the heat and cook for a further 2 minutes, stirring constantly.

Mix the tagliatelle into the mushroom mixture with most of the coriander, reserving some for garnish. Season to taste. Divide the pasta between warmed wide-rimmed bowls and arrange two chicken legs on top of each serving. Garnish with the remaining coriander and serve at once.

Nutritional value per serving:

Calories: 773

Fats: 38g

Carbohydrates: 56g

Salt: 0.69g

Saturated fat: 1.1g

Fibre: 2.9g

oven-baked **bream** with root vegetables

450g (1lb) sweet potatoes, peeled and cut
 into chunks

450g (1lb) potatoes, peeled and cut into chunks

450g (1lb) smallish yellow onions, skinned and
 quartered

450g (1lb) ripe firm tomatoes, cut into chunks

1 glass dry white wine

4 tablespoons olive oil

1 sea bream, weighing about 900g (2lb) when
 cleaned, head left on

rough salt

chilli flakes

Arrange the vegetables in a roasting tin, pour in the wine, trickle with the oil and finish with liberal dusting of salt and chilli flakes. Cover with foil, shiny-side down. Bake for 20 minutes, until the vegetables are nearly tender. Carefully remove the foil. Place the fish on the bed of vegetables, sprinkle with salt and chilli flakes, replace the foil and bake for another 10 minutes, until the fish is cooked right through. It's ready when it feels firm to your finger. Remove and leave on one side for another 10 minutes, so that the heat can penetrate right through to the bone.

Nutritional value per serving:

Calories: 510

Fats: 17g

Carbohydrates: 48g

Salt: 1.05g

Saturated fat: 2.8g

Fibre: 6.1g

monkfish with pine nuts & sultanas

700g (1½lb) monkfish tail

600 ml (1 pint) water

6 black peppercorns

1 large Spanish onion, peeled and finely sliced

3 tablespoons of olive oil

50 g (2oz) sultanas

1 teaspoon saffron strands

175ml (6fl oz) fruity white wine

50g (2oz) pine nuts

sea salt

Cut the monkfish off the tail bone (reserve this for stock) and slice the flesh into large chunks about 5cm (2in) square. Pour the measured water into a pan, add the tail bone, and with the peppercorns simmer actively for 20 minutes to make a light stock. Strain the stock and pour over the sultanas. Leave to stand for 15 minutes then drain, reserving 175ml (6fl oz) of the liquid. Place the saffron to steep in this liquid.

In a large heavy pan, heat the olive oil over a medium heat and add the onion. Fry for 10 minutes, stirring frequently, until golden.

Turn the heat up to medium high and add the monkfish pieces to the pan. Fry for 3-4 minutes, turning several times, until slightly golden. Now add the wine to the pan and allow to bubble fiercely for 1 minute. Add the saffron liquid, the sultanas and pine nuts and a good pinch of salt. Bring to the boil then turn the heat to low and leave to simmer for 10 minutes. Check seasoning before serving.

Nutritional value per serving:

Calories: 378

Fats: 19g

Carbohydrates: 18g

Salt: 0.34g

Saturated fat: 2.6g

Fibre: 1.6g

fillet of brill with cucumber spaghetti & herb crème fraîche

200g (7oz) crème fraîche

juice of ¹/₂ lemon

1 tablespoon chopped mixed herbs (such as dill, chervil and chives)

2 cucumbers

2 large carrots

2 tablespoons olive oil

4 x 150g (5oz) brill fillets, unskinned

Place the crème fraîche in a bowl and add the lemon juice (reserving half a teaspoon) and the herbs. Season to taste and mix well, then cover with cling film and place in the fridge to firm up. (This can be made the day before and left in the fridge overnight.)

Peel each cucumber, then cut in half and remove the seeds with a teaspoon; discard. Slice the cucumbers on a mandolin into long thin strips so that it resembles 'spaghetti' and place in a bowl. Peel the carrots and slice on the mandolin just like the cucumbers. Add to the cucumbers and gently mix to combine the colours. Add the reserved half a teaspoon of lemon juice, one teaspoon of the oil and season generously, mixing gently to combine. Cover with cling film and set aside to allow the flavours to mingle.

Heat a non-stick frying pan until very hot. Add the remaining olive oil to the pan and then add the brill fillets, skin-side down. Cook for 4-5 minutes, until the skin is crisp and golden, then turn over and cook for another minute until tender. Season to taste.

Arrange the cucumber spaghetti in wide-rimmed bowls and place a piece of brill on top of each one. Quickly dip two tablespoons into boiling water and use to shape the herb crème fraîche into a quenelle - you will probably have some left-over that can be used for another dish. Place one on each piece of brill and serve immediately with cumin-roasted new potatoes, if liked.

Nutritional value per serving:

Calories: 397

Fats: 24g

Carbohydrates: 10g

Salt: 0.41g

Saturated fat: 11g

Fibre: 2.6g

rice with **squid** & mussels

900g (2lb) mussels, cleaned and scrubbed
   (discarding any open ones that don't close
   on being tapped)

4 tablespoons olive oil

800g (1¾lb) squid, cleaned and cut into
   tablespoon-sized pieces

2 garlic cloves, finely chopped

400g (14oz) Valencia rice (or a risotto rice)

1 x 400g (14oz) tin chopped tomatoes

1 litre (1¾ pint) hot chicken stock

pinch of saffron threads, dissolved in a little
   hot water

1 tablespoon chopped parsley

3-4 lemons, halved

salt and freshly ground black pepper

Put the mussels in a saucepan, cover with a lid and place over a moderate heat, shaking well. The mussels take 4-5 minutes to open. Remove the lid and set aside to cool.

Heat the olive oil in a flameproof casserole. Season the squid with salt and sauté for 5 minutes. Stir in the garlic and rice and sauté for 2 minutes. Add the tomatoes with their liquid and the stock. Bring to the boil, stir once and simmer for 20 minutes.

Meanwhile, remove the mussels from their shells, leaving a dozen or so intact for decoration. (Any mussels that have not opened should be discarded.) Strain the liquor from the saucepan, taking care to leave any grit behind. A couple of minutes before the end of rice cooking time, stir in the strained liquor and the mussels along with the saffron and its soaking liquid. Adjust the seasoning, stir in the parsley and serve with a lemon half.

How to debeard mussels

To remove the beards from mussels, hold the mussel with the pointed end away from you. Pull downwards on the beard to remove it. Scrub the mussels well before cooking.

Nutritional value per serving:

Calories: 457

Fats: 11g

Carbohydrates: 59g

Salt: 1.69g

Saturated fat: 1.3g

Fibre: 1.8g

SERVES 4

PREPARATION TIME: 15 MINUTES

COOKING TIME: 45 MINUTES

prawn & feta risotto

1.2 litres (2 pints) vegetable stock
50g (2oz) small peeled cooked prawns
1 red chilli, deseeded and finely chopped
4 tablespoons olive oil
1 x 250g (9oz) tin of tomatoes, drained
good pinch of dried oregano
50g (2oz) butter
1 onion, finely chopped
4 whole celery stalks, finely chopped
2 carrots, finely chopped
3 garlic cloves, finely chopped
250g (9oz) Arborio rice
1/2 bottle of good white wine
110g (4oz) feta cheese
salt and freshly ground black pepper

Rocket & cucumber salad
85g (3oz) rocket leaves
1 cucumber, chopped
2 tablespoons olive oil
juice of 1 lemon

Put the vegetable stock in a saucepan and bring to the boil. While the stock is heating, sauté the prawns and finely chopped chilli in 3 tablespoons of the olive oil until golden, then pull off the heat. Purée the tinned tomatoes with a little oregano and the remaining olive oil, and place to one side.

Gently melt the butter in a large flameproof casserole and add the onion, celery, carrots and garlic. Sweat gently for 10 minutes until softened. Now add the Arborio rice and stir for 3 minutes. Pour in the white wine and cook, stirring from time to time, until the rice mixture becomes firm.

Slowly start to add the simmering vegetable stock to the rice, 150ml (1/4 pint) at a time every 2-3 minutes, stirring occasionally. Once all the stock has been added, gently stir in the puréed tomatoes, then crumble in the feta cheese. Add the parsley followed by the cooked prawns. Season to taste with salt and pepper.

Make the salad by tossing the rocket leaves and cucumber with the oil, lemon juice and seasoning to taste. Serve the risotto with the salad.

Nutritional value per serving:
Calories: 654
Fats: 33g
Carbohydrates: 61g
Salt: 3.24g
Saturated fat: 12.2g
Fibre: 4.7g

SERVES 4

PREPARATION TIME: 15 MINUTES

COOKING TIME: 50 MINUTES

roast chump of lamb with garlic

600g (1¼lb) new potatoes, scrubbed and cut
 into 1cm (½in) slices
4 tablespoons olive oil
6 garlic cloves, finely chopped
2 teaspoons fresh thyme leaves
4 x 175g (6oz) lamb chumps
2 courgettes, cut into rough triangles
4 ripe, firm tomatoes, quartered

Preheat the oven to 180°C/350°F/gas mark 4. Place the potatoes in a large roasting tin with two tablespoons of the olive oil and season generously. Toss to coat and roast for 20 minutes, then add the garlic and thyme, tossing again to coat and roast for another 8-10 minutes or until the potatoes are crisp and tender. Leave the garlic and thyme juices in the roasting tin.

Meanwhile, heat a heavy-based roasting tin on the hob. Season the lamb chumps.

Add the remaining two tablespoons of olive oil to the tin and then add the lamb chumps. Sear on each side for a minute or so until well sealed and golden brown in patches. Place each chump skin-side down and roast for 10-12 minutes until just tender but still slightly pink in the middle. Transfer to a warmed dish and leave to rest in a warm place.

Add the courgettes to the same roasting tin with the remaining garlic and thyme, tossing to coat in the juices and roast for 5 minutes. Add the tomatoes, tossing again to coat and cook for another 5 minutes, remembering to turn the vegetables occasionally.

Meanwhile, arrange the potatoes on warmed serving plates and spoon over the cooked vegetables. Carve the lamb and arrange on top, then drizzle all of the meat and vegetable juices on top as a sauce. Serve immediately.

Nutritional value per serving:
Calories: 615
Fats: 41g
Carbohydrates: 31g
Salt: 0.27g
Saturated fat: 16.5g
Fibre: 3.7g

lamb & apricot tagine

110g (4oz) dried apricots

450 g (1lb) shoulder of lamb, off the bone,
    trimmed of fat and cut into chunks

1 teaspoon powdered ginger

1 teaspoon ground cinnamon

2 teaspoon freshly ground black pepper

pinch of mace or nutmeg

1 large onion, peeled and grated

50g (2oz) unsalted butter, cut into small pieces

1 small bunch fresh coriander

1 small bunch fresh flat-leaf parsley

sea salt

Pour sufficient boiling water over the apricots to just cover them and leave to soak. Place the meat in a large heavy casserole or better still a tagine if you have one. Sprinkle over the spices, the grated onion and the butter. Place the casserole over a low heat and cook for 5 minutes, stirring regularly, until the butter melts and the spices give off their scent – the meat should not brown. Tie the herbs together in a bunch and add them to the pot. Pour in just enough water to barely cover the meat. Bring to the boil then turn down the heat and leave to simmer gently for 1 hour.

Now add the apricots to the tagine, together with their liquid and salt to taste. Cook for a further 30 minutes, until the apricots are plumped up. Taste to check the seasoning, remove the bunches of herbs and serve with flat bread.

How to make herb bouquet

Gather the herb stalks together and tie tightly with kitchen string. Secure the ends tightly.

Nutritional value per serving:

Calories: 346

Fats: 19g

Carbohydrates: 19g

Salt: 0.5g

Saturated fat: 10.5g

Fibre: 2.9g

shoulder of **lamb** with yogurt & cardamom

1.8kg (4lb) shoulder of lamb, boned
    and rolled
4 garlic cloves, cut into slivers
4 tablespoons cardamom pods
3 tablespoons olive oil
juice and grated zest of 1 lemon
¼ teaspoon saffron strands
150g (5oz) Greek yogurt
2 tablespoons brown sugar
salt and freshly ground black pepper

Season the lamb with salt and pepper and make deep cuts in it with a sharp knife. Insert the garlic slivers into the cuts. Crush the cardamom pods, then sprinkle over the cardamom seeds and rub them in. Leave at room temperature for 5 hours (or overnight in the fridge). Preheat the oven to 200°C/400°F/gas mark 6. Heat the oil in a roasting tin, add the lamb and brown all over. Transfer to the oven and roast for 20-30 minutes, until well coloured. Remove from the oven and leave to cool slightly while you prepare the lemon yogurt coating. Reduce the oven to 170°C/325°F/gas mark 3. Put the lemon juice and saffron in a small pan and heat gently. Leave to cool, then mix with the lemon zest, yogurt and sugar. Pour half this mixture over the lamb. Return the lamb to the oven and cook, adding more lemon yogurt every 30 minutes or so, for about 2½-3 hours, until the lamb is very tender and is topped with a golden yogurt crust. Allow to cool slightly before serving.

How to grind cardamom pods
Grinding cardamom pods in a pestle and mortar releases the small black seeds from inside the pods.

Nutritional value per serving:
Calories: 620
Fats: 46g
Carbohydrates: 8g
Salt: 0.56g
Saturated fat: 21.4g
Fibre: 0.1g

SERVES 4

PREPARATION TIME: 10 MINUTES

COOKING TIME: 1½ HOURS

MARINATING TIME: 24 HOURS

braised rabbit with bacon, tomato & broad beans

1 young rabbit (about 1.6kg/3½ lb), jointed

2 tablespoons plain flour

2 tablespoons olive oil

25g (1oz) unsalted butter

75g (3oz) smoked bacon lardons

150ml (¼ pint) dry white wine

300ml (½ pint) well-flavoured meat stock

75g (3oz) sun-blushed tomatoes

50g (2oz) shelled broad beans, cooked

salt and freshly ground black pepper

Marinade

12 garlic cloves, peeled but left whole

1 small bay leaf

6 rosemary sprigs, plus extra to garnish

2 tablespoons olive oil

Put the rabbit joints in a dish with all the marinade ingredients. Cover and leave to marinate for 24 hours.

Preheat the oven to 150°C/300°F/gas mark 2. Remove the rabbit from the marinade and dry well, then coat it in the flour. Heat the olive oil and the butter in a large casserole until very hot, then season the rabbit joints and brown them in the hot fat. Add the garlic cloves from the marinade and the smoked bacon and cook for 3-4 minutes. Drain off any excess fat, then return to the heat, pour in the white wine and tuck in the rosemary sprigs and bay leaf from the marinade. Pour over the meat stock and bring to the boil. Reduce the heat, cover and place in the oven. Cook for 1 hour, then add the sun-blushed tomatoes and cook for 15 minutes longer.

Remove from the oven and strain off the liquid into a saucepan. Simmer until it is thick enough to coat the back of a spoon, then stir in the broad beans and season to taste. Pour the sauce over the rabbit, garnish with a little rosemary and serve. Creamy mashed potato, lightened with olive oil, makes a good accompaniment.

Nutritional value per serving:

Calories: 593

Fats: 32g

Carbohydrates: 12g

Salt: 2.12g

Saturated fat: 11.7g

Fibre: 0.8g

persian **beef** stew

110g (4oz) yellow split peas

1 tablespoon extra-virgin olive oil

1 large onion, finely chopped

350g (12oz) lean stewing beef, trimmed of
  fat and cubed

1 teaspoon ground cinnamon

¼ teaspoon grated nutmeg

600ml (1 pint) beef stock

1 large cooking apple, peeled, cored and
  thickly sliced

1 sweet potato, peeled and cubed

juice of 1 lemon

2 tablespoons runny honey

75g (3oz) raisins

110g (4oz) frozen peas

salt and freshly ground black pepper

Put the split peas in a bowl, cover with water, and leave for 1 hour.

Heat the oil in a large, deep frying pan, add the onion and soften gently for 3 minutes. Add the meat and continue cooking, stirring continuously, until the meat is sealed and the onion becomes slightly golden. Stir in the cinnamon and nutmeg, add the stock and simmer, covered, for 30 minutes.

Drain and rinse the split peas. Put into a saucepan of boiling water and boil for 5 minutes. Drain. Add the split peas to the pan with the apple and potato. Bring back to the boil, cover and simmer for 15 minutes.

Add the lemon juice, honey, raisins and green peas, pushing the raisins and the peas into the pan without breaking up the apple. Continue to simmer for 15-20 minutes. Season with salt and pepper if necessary, and serve.

Nutritional value per serving:

Calories: 405

Fats: 9g

Carbohydrates: 55g

Salt: 0.99g

Saturated fat: 2.7g

Fibre: 5.8g

SERVES 4

PREPARATION TIME: 10 MINUTES

COOKING TIME: 2 HOURS

SOAKING TIME: 6-12 HOURS

calf's liver & bacon with puy lentils

4 tablespoons olive oil

200g (7oz) smoked bacon, cut into strips

2 cloves garlic, crushed

20 baby onions

100g (3½oz) Puy lentils, soaked for 24 hours

600ml (1 pint) chicken stock

375g (13oz) calf's liver, sliced

4 tablespoons balsamic vinegar

4 tablespoons chopped parsley

salt and freshly ground black pepper

Pour half the oil into a large sauté pan and sauté the smoked bacon, garlic and onions until golden brown. Add the soaked lentils and add to the pan with the chicken stock. Leave to simmer for 1½-2 hours.

Towards the end of the cooking time, pour the rest of the oil into a second large sauté pan over a moderately high heat. Season the liver and seal in the hot oil on both sides, then transfer to the pan containing the lentils.

Cook the liver with the lentils for another 10 minutes. Mix in the balsamic vinegar and serve sprinkled with chopped parsley.

Nutritional value per serving:

Calories: 410

Fats: 23g

Carbohydrates: 16g

Salt: 2.9g

Saturated fat: 5.8g

Fibre: 3.3g

layered fajitas

Fajitas

175g (6oz) plain flour

good pinch of salt

corn oil, for frying

Filling

2 x 400g (14oz) tins of red beans (or 200g/7oz
  dried beans soaked for 24 hours)

2 tablespoons corn oil

1 onion, chopped

1 red chilli, deseeded and chopped

1 garlic clove, chopped

$\frac{1}{2}$ bunch of fresh coriander, chopped

dash of Tabasco sauce

juice of 1 lime

125ml (4fl oz) sour cream

Salsa

4 tomatoes, deseeded and chopped

$\frac{1}{2}$ bunch of fresh coriander (stalks and all),
  chopped

$\frac{1}{2}$ red onion, chopped

3 tablespoons corn oil

Nutritional value per serving:

Calories: 530

Fats: 22g

Carbohydrates: 65g

Salt: 1.6g

Saturated fat: 5.9g

Fibre: 10.8g

First make the fajitas: pour the flour and salt into a mixing bowl, make a well in the centre and add 300ml ($\frac{1}{2}$ pint) water. Mix together, adding a little more water, if necessary, until you have a firm dough. Knead the dough until nice and smooth, then cut into 6 pieces and shape into balls. Roll each ball out to a 17.5cm (7in) round. Heat a non-stick frying pan and dry-fry each fajita on both sides until it puffs up and immediately remove from the heat.

Make the filling: if using soaked dried beans, drain them, add to a pot of boiling water and cook gently for 2 hours; if using tinned beans, drain and add to a pot with 300 ml ($\frac{1}{2}$ pint) water and cook gently for 30 minutes.

Add the corn oil to a saucepan and cook the onion, chilli and garlic until softened. Add the drained beans and cook for a further 10 minutes, stirring, then start to mash the beans roughly with the back of a fork, adding the chopped coriander, a dash of Tabasco and the lime juice. Stir well and pull from heat.

Make the salsa by mixing together all the ingredients.

Lay each fajita on a plate, spoon over a quarter of the bean filling, add a dollop of sour cream, drizzle with a little salsa and repeat layering your 5 fajitas until you come to the final fajita which you use as a lid, pressing down firmly. Top with the remaining salsa, place in the fridge and allow to set. Cut into pie wedges and eat outdoors.

TIP

If you like, you can add a deseeded and chopped red chilli to the salsa for some authentic chilli heat.

fresh bean cassoulet with garlic polenta wedges

400ml (²/₃ pint) water or vegetable stock

90g (3¹/₄oz) polenta

1 clove garlic, crushed

¹/₂ teaspoon dried mixed herbs

1 dessertspoon extra virgin olive oil

1 onion, finely chopped

1 clove garlic, crushed

1 carrot, sliced

25g (1oz) fennel, roughly chopped

75g (3oz) mushrooms, sliced

3 sprigs rosemary

1 bay leaf and 1 sprig thyme

1 x 400g (14oz) can cannellini beans, drained

110g (4oz) broad beans

110g (4oz) runner beans, sliced diagonally

300ml (¹/₂ pint) vegetable stock

1 dessertspoon soy sauce

1 teaspoon cornflour, mixed with a little water

sea salt and freshly ground black pepper

Bring the stock to the boil in a large pan. Add the polenta to the stock slowly, stirring continuously. When the mixture starts to thicken, add the garlic and mixed herbs and season. Continue to stir until the mixture resembles a smooth porridge, 4-5 minutes. Turn the polenta into a round, non-stick tin, smooth the surface and set aside to cool.

Sweat the onion and garlic with the olive oil in a covered pan for 3-4 minutes. Add the carrot, fennel, mushrooms and herbs to the pan and sweat for another 6-7 minutes. Add the beans and stock to the pan and bring to the boil. Simmer for 15-20 minutes. When the beans are tender, add the soy sauce and cornflour mixture to the pan and simmer for about 5 minutes more to thicken the sauce. Season. Grill the polenta wedges until crisp and brown and serve hot with the cassoulet.

How to cook and grill polenta

Pour cooked polenta into a greased round tin. Leave until cold then cut into triangles. Heat a ridged grill pan, oil each piece of polenta and fry until chargrilled.

Nutritional value per serving:

Calories: 459

Fats: 9g

Carbohydrates: 77g

Salt: 2.93g

Saturated fat: 1g

Fibre: 15.1g

vegetable bake

6 tablespoons olive oil

3 sweet Spanish onions, diced

2 garlic cloves, finely chopped

3 large sprigs fresh oregano, roughly chopped.

2 smallish aubergines, cut into 5mm (¼in) slices

5 courgettes, peeled if necessary and cut into 5mm (¼in) slices

6 tomatoes, cut into 5mm (¼in) slices

450g (1lb) fresh, young mozzarella cheese, cut into 5mm (¼in) slices

5 tablespoons freshly grated Parmesan

6 sprigs dill

freshly ground black pepper

Preheat the oven to 200°C/400°F/gas mark 6.

Heat the oil in a frying pan, add the onions and cook gently for 5 minutes to soften. Add the garlic and continue cooking for 3 minutes. Stir the oregano into the onion mixture and remove from the heat.

Put the aubergine slices on a baking tray in a single layer, sprinkle with salt and bake for 8 minutes until softened.

Put the onion and herb mixture into an ovenproof dish. Arrange the aubergine, courgette, tomato and mozzarella alternately in the dish, standing them on their sides. When they're all arranged, push down gently with the palms of your hands and season with black pepper. Place the dish in the oven and bake for about 1 hour. Sprinkle the Parmesan on top and bake for another 10 minutes.

Serve with the whole sprigs of dill scattered on top.

TIP

Fresh oregano is widely available. Dried won't be as good for aroma or flavour, but if you have to use it, add 1 tablespoon.

Nutritional value per serving:

Calories: 667

Fats: 46g

Carbohydrates: 25g

Salt: 2.14g

Saturated fat: 20.4g

Fibre: 7.8g

bean, **pumpkin** & sweetcorn casserole

450g (1lb) fresh, shelled beans

450g (1lb) piece pumpkin, skinned and chunked

1 tablespoon soft pork lard or oil

1 link soft chorizo, crumbled (or 4 slices
   bacon, diced)

2 large mild onions, finely chopped

1 red pepper, deseeded and diced

1 carrot, scraped and coarsely grated

600ml (1 pint) fresh corn kernels

handful fresh basil leaves, chopped

salt

To finish

2 garlic cloves, skinned and roughly chopped

1 tablespoon paprika

pinch of powdered chilli

1-2 tablespoons oil

salt

Put the shelled beans and the pumpkin in a roomy pot, add enough hot water to cover to a depth of two fingers, bring to the boil, reduce the heat, put the lid on and simmer until the pumpkin has melted to a soupy sauce and the beans are perfectly tender: 40-60 minutes.

Meanwhile, heat the lard or oil gently in a small frying pan and fry the chorizo or diced bacon until it takes a little colour. Add the onion, red pepper and carrot, salt lightly and fry until soft and a little caramelised. Stir into the beans and simmer for another 10 minutes.

Meanwhile, put the corn kernels in the liquidiser with a ladleful of the bean liquor and the basil leaves (reserve a few of the best). Process to a purée, stir into the beans and simmer for another 15 minutes – dilute with a little boiling water if it looks too thick.

To make the finishing oil, crush the garlic cloves with a little salt and work in the oil and spices. Serve in deep earthenware bowls, with a swirl of scarlet oil and a basil leaf to finish.

Nutritional value per serving:

Calories: 416

Fats: 17g

Carbohydrates: 50g

Salt: 0.9g

Saturated fat: 4.7g

Fibre: 12.5g

spinach greens with peanuts

700g (1½lb) spinach greens or other leaves
½ teaspoon salt
450g (1lb) tomatoes, finely chopped
6-8 spring onions, finely chopped
4 tablespoons pounded roasted peanuts

Cook the spinach in a tightly lidded pan in the water which clings to the leaves after washing. Sprinkle with salt to encourage the juices to run.

As soon as the leaves collapse and soften, remove the lid and add a layer of chopped tomatoes and chopped spring onion. Sprinkle with the powdered peanuts, but do not stir. Turn down the heat, put the lid on loosely and simmer for about 15 minutes, until the tomato flesh has softened. Stir, put the lid on loosely again and simmer for another 15 minutes. Remove the lid and bubble up to evaporate any excess juices. Reverse the contents of the pan onto the serving dish, and finish with a sprinkle of whole roast peanuts.

TIP
A Brazilian dish of African origin, this dish can be made with a wide variety of edible greens including spinach of the tough evergreen variety, the young leaves of pumpkin, cassava and sweet potato, chard, spring greens and cabbage. Serve as a vegetarian dish with soft polenta or rice.

Nutritional value per serving:

Calories: 138

Fats: 8g

Carbohydrates: 7g

Salt: 1.4g

Saturated fat: 1.5g

Fibre: 5.7g

butter beans with pumpkin

225g (8oz) butter beans (limas), soaked
   overnight
450g (1lb) yellow-fleshed potatoes, peeled and
   cubed in bite-sized pieces
450g (1lb) pumpkin or any winter squash, cubed
   in bite-sized pieces
600ml (1 pint) fresh or frozen sweetcorn
salt
chopped parsley, to serve
crumbled white cheese such as feta, to serve

Flavouring salsa
3 yellow chillies, deseeded and chopped
1 small yellow onion, finely chopped
6 spring onions, finely chopped with their green
3 garlic cloves, finely chopped
2 tablespoons olive oil

Cook the beans in a roomy pot with enough water to cover. Don't put the lid on. The water should tremble but never come off the boil. Allow 2 hours (1 hour if the beans are fresh) and cook until soft but not mushy. Add boiling water as and when necessary, but no salt.

Meanwhile, bubble up the salsa ingredients in a small pan, and set aside to combine the flavours.

When the beans are tender, add the vegetables and extra boiling water, salt and the prepared salsa, and cook for another half hour, until the vegetables are perfectly soft. The dish should be moist but not soupy. Finish with a handful of chopped parsley and crumbled white cheese – feta is the right texture.

Nutritional value per serving:
Calories: 478
Fats: 12g
Carbohydrates: 76g
Salt: 0.79g
Saturated fat: 2.9g
Fibre: 14.2g

chargrilled **polenta** with roasted red & yellow peppers

1.8 litres (3 pints) water

2 teaspoons salt

225g (8oz) coarse polenta

6 tablespoons olive tapenade

3 red peppers

3 yellow peppers

sea salt and freshly ground pepper

Put the water into a deep saucepan and bring to the boil, add salt, then sprinkle the polenta in slowly, whisking all the time (this should take 3-4 minutes). Bring to the boil and when it starts to 'erupt like a volcano' turn the heat down to the absolute minimum and cook for about 40 minutes, stirring regularly. The polenta is cooked when it is very thick but not solid and comes away from the sides of the pot as you stir. As soon as the polenta is cooked, season with lots of pepper. Taste and add a little more sea salt if necessary. Pour the cooked polenta into a wet dish (use a lasagne dish: 23 x 18 x 5cm (9 x 7 x 2in) which is just perfect for this quantity, but you could use a Swiss roll tin and cut it into squares or diamonds when it is cold). Allow to get completely cold.

Preheat the oven to 250°C/475°F/gas mark 9. Put the peppers on a baking tray and bake for 20-30 minutes until the skin blisters and the flesh is soft. Put them into a bowl and cover tightly with cling film for a few minutes; this will make them much easier to peel. Pull the skin off the peppers, remove the stalks and seeds. Do not wash or you will lose the precious sweet juices. Divide each into 2 or 3 pieces along the natural division.

To serve: cut the polenta into slices 1-2cm ($^1/_2$-$^3/_4$in) thick and chargrill, pan-grill or fry. Put it directly on to the bars of the grill on the highest heat without oil and cook until it is hot through and grill-marked on each side. Spread a spoonful of tapenade on to each slice and top with the roasted red and yellow peppers.

Nutritional value per serving:

Calories: 249

Fats: 9g

Carbohydrates: 36g

Salt: 2.24g

Saturated fat: 0.9g

Fibre: 1.5g

outdoor
food

salt-griddled prawns with lime & garlic

20 extra-large uncooked tiger prawns, shell on

4 tablespoons virgin olive oil

juice of $1/4$ lemon

$1/2$ teaspoon chopped thyme

$1/2$ teaspoon chopped oregano

2 tablespoons coarse salt

$1/4$ teaspoon garlic salt

freshly ground black pepper

Lime and garlic sauce

200ml (7fl oz) fish stock

juice of 3 limes

grated zest of 1 lime

1 garlic clove, crushed

1 small red onion, finely chopped

2 tablespoons chopped flat-leaf parsley

25g (1oz) chilled unsalted butter, diced

Cut down the back of each prawn shell with a sharp knife or kitchen scissors and lift out the black intestinal vein, leaving the shell on. Coat the prawns in the olive oil and lemon juice and season with black pepper. In a bowl, mix together the herbs and salts. Dredge the prawns in the mixture, ensuring they are well coated. Grill the salt-crusted prawns on a hot barbecue or a ridged grill pan for 3-4 minutes on each side.

Meanwhile, make the sauce. Put all the ingredients except the butter in a pan and bring to the boil. Remove from the heat and whisk in the butter.

Remove the prawns from the barbecue and arrange on a serving dish. Pour the sauce around them and serve.

Nutritional value per serving:

Calories: 253

Fats: 17g

Carbohydrates: 2g

Salt: 4.52g

Saturated fat: 4.8g

Fibre: 0.4g

squid ink pasta with prawn salad

30 fresh medium tiger prawns, peeled
olive oil
500g (1lb 2oz) fresh squid ink tagliatelle
30 asparagus spears, peeled and blanched
1 bunch of spring onions, washed, roots
    trimmed, finely sliced
10 plum tomatoes, skinned, deseeded and diced
2 red chillies, deseeded and finely sliced
$1/2$ tea cup snipped chives
salt and freshly ground black pepper

Dressing
3 tablespoons white wine vinegar
1 tablespoon caster sugar
5 tablespoons extra-virgin olive oil

First make the dressing: blend the vinegar and sugar in a blender or food processor for 20 seconds. Add the oil slowly in a steady stream until emulsified.

Preheat the barbecue or grill pan. Brush the prawns with olive oil, season, place on the barbecue and cook evenly on all sides. Bring a saucepan of salted water with a little olive oil to the boil, cook the pasta al dente, drain and refresh.

Place the prawns, pasta and asparagus in a large bowl and pour over the dressing. Add the spring onions, tomatoes, chillies and chives; toss well. Season and serve.

Nutritional value per serving:
Calories: 244
Fats: 8g
Carbohydrates: 31g
Salt: 0.45g
Saturated fat: 1g
Fibre: 2.5g

dressed sardines

12 fresh (as fresh as possible) sardines

25g (1oz) plain flour

a little olive oil, for coating

Dressing

large bunch of mint, finely shredded

2 tablespoons red wine vinegar

pinch of celery salt

2 shallots, finely chopped

grated zest of 2 lemons

pinch of dried chillies

2 tablespoons olive oil

salt and freshly ground black pepper

First prepare the dressing: in a bowl, mix the mint, vinegar, celery salt, chopped shallots, lemon zest and chilli. Place to one side.

Run a sharp knife along the underside (belly) of the sardine. Under very gentle running water, using the best kitchen tool of all, the index finger, remove the fish's innards. At this point, still under running water, gently scrape off any outer scales from the fish, ensuring you remove all of them – they come away easily using your thumb or a table knife. Using a tea towel, dry the sardines well to help avoid their sticking to the grill.

Pour the flour on to one large plate and drizzle a little olive oil on another. Dip the sardines into the flour on both sides to coat, and then lightly pull the fish through the olive oil. Place on the preheated hot barbecue and cook them for about 5 minutes on each side.

Finish the dressing by adding the oil and seasoning with salt and pepper. Lay the cooked sardines on a large plate and spoon over the delicious fresh, tangy dressing – the perfect accompaniment for sardines.

Nutritional value per serving:

Calories: 422

Fats: 25g

Carbohydrates: 7g

Salt: 1.13g

Saturated fat: 4.7g

Fibre: 0.3g

SERVES 4

PREPARATION TIME: 15 MINUTES

COOKING TIME: 20 MINUTES

MARINATING TIME: 1 HOUR

chargrilled **tuna** with green papaya salad

650g (1lb 7oz) small tuna fillet, trimmed

2 tablespoons tamarind paste

2 tablespoons brown sugar

2 red chillies, deseeded and finely chopped

1 tablespoon *nam pla* (Thai fish sauce)

oil for grilling

salt and freshly ground black pepper

1 lime, cut into wedges, to garnish

Green papaya salad

1 garlic clove, chopped

2 red chillies, deseeded and chopped

1 teaspoon brown sugar

2 green papayas, peeled, deseeded and
   shredded

juice of 2 limes

2 tablespoons *nam pla* (Thai fish sauce)

100g (3$\frac{1}{2}$ oz) French beans, cooked

2 tablespoons roasted peanuts

10 red cherry tomatoes, halved

10 yellow cherry tomatoes, halved

Nutritional value per serving:

Calories: 398

Fats: 12g

Carbohydrates: 32g

Salt: 2.59g

Saturated fat: 3.2g

Fibre: 4.9g

Cut the tuna into 4 steaks across the fillet. In a bowl, combine the tamarind with the sugar, chillies, fish sauce and some salt and pepper. Pour this mixture over the tuna and set aside for 1 hour to allow the flavours to meld.

For the salad, roughly crush the garlic, chillies, sugar and a quarter of the shredded papaya in a mortar. Transfer to a bowl, add the lime juice and fish sauce and stir well. Add all the remaining ingredients, including the rest of the papaya, toss well and season to taste. Barbecue the tuna steaks or pangrill them as shown below. Remove from the grill and cut each steak into 4 slices. Arrange a pile of salad on each serving plate, top with the seared tuna, then garnish with the lime wedges and serve.

How to chargrill tuna steaks

Heat a ridged grill pan until very hot. Brush the tuna steaks with a little oil and season with salt and pepper. Chargrill for 2 minutes on each side, keeping them rare.

spiedinos of scallops, monkfish & pancetta

1 ciabatta loaf, cut into 12 cubes
4 tablespoons extra-virgin olive oil
12 slices of pancetta or smoked back bacon
12 shelled scallops, preferably with their corals
900g (2lb) monkfish tail, cut into 12 cubes
juice of 1–2 lemon(s), to serve
salt and freshly ground black pepper
6 stout fennel sticks or long skewers (about
    25cm/10in long)

Put the ciabatta chunks in a large mixing bowl, pour over the olive oil and stir around well. Remove each chunk of bread and wrap a strip of pancetta around it. Then taking a skewer, first spear one piece of wrapped bread (skewering the pancetta-wrapped side to ensure it doesn't fall off during cooking), then spear a scallop through the coral and then the white meat lengthways, then skewer a chunk of monkfish. Repeat this until you have 6 pieces, two of each ingredient on each skewer.

Lightly season the spiedinos, place on the hottest part of the barbecue and grill for 10 minutes on each side. Serve on a large plate with a squeeze of lemon juice.

How to prepare scallops

With the flat side of the scallop upwards, slide a sharp knife between the two halves of the shell to cut the nerve holding them closed. Remove and discard the top shell. Slide the knife underneath the exposed scallop and ease it off the shell. Discard the black tissue around it and cut off the black vein that runs around the side of the scallop.

Nutritional value per serving:
Calories: 406
Fats: 18g
Carbohydrates: 20g
Salt: 2.5g
Saturated fat: 4.7g
Fibre: 1.1g

grilled spiced spring **chicken**

2 small spring chickens or poussins,
   spatchcocked
4 tablespoons olive oil
juice of 1 lemon
1 teaspoon paprika
3 teaspoons coarse sea salt
1 teaspoon ground cumin
1 teaspoon cayenne pepper
2 tablespoons finely chopped fresh flat-leaf
   parsley
toasted cumin seeds

Mix together all the marinade ingredients and pour over the chickens. Leave for at least 2 hours.

Meanwhile, get the barbecue coals glowing and heat a ridged grill pan, or heat the grill to maximum. Grill the chickens for 25-30 minutes, placing them skin side down on the barbecue or grill pan and skin side up under the grill. Turn the chickens to expose the underside to the heat after 10 minutes and turn back after another 10 minutes so that you finish skin side to the heat source. Baste regularly with the marinade. Serve with quartered lemons and bowls of coarse sea salt and toasted cumin seeds.

Nutritional value per serving:
Calories: 797
Fats: 56g
Carbohydrates: 1g
Salt: 2.42g
Saturated fat: 0.4g
Fibre: 0.1g

grilled chicken with sweet chilli sauce

Marinade

2 tablespoons sesame oil

2 garlic cloves, finely chopped

1 teaspoon finely chopped coriander root

2 small fresh red chillies, finely chopped

2 tablespoons *nam pla* (Thai fish sauce)

1 teaspoon granulated sugar

400g (14oz) boneless chicken breasts, with skin, cut into chunks

Hot and sweet sauce

6 tablespoons rice or white wine vinegar

4 tablespoons granulated sugar

$1/2$ teaspoon salt

2 garlic cloves, finely chopped

3 small fresh red chillies, finely chopped

In a large bowl, mix together all the ingredients for the marinade and leave to marinate for 30 minutes.

Meanwhile, make the hot and sweet sauce. In a small saucepan, heat the vinegar and sugar and stir until dissolved. Add the salt and simmer, stirring, until the liquid thickens. Remove from the heat, pour into a small bowl and leave to cool. When the sauce is cold, stir in the chopped garlic and chillies.

Barbecue the marinated chicken for about 5 minutes on each side, or until cooked through.

Arrange the chicken on a platter and serve with the bowl of sauce.

Nutritional value per serving:

Calories: 238

Fats: 8g

Carbohydrates: 20g

Salt: 2.38g

Saturated fat: 1.7g

Fibre: 0.4g

lamb kebabs with tzatziki

900g (2lb) lean shoulder or leg of lamb

Marinade
300ml (½ pint) natural yogurt
1 teaspoon ground coriander
1 teaspoon ground cumin
¼ teaspoon freshly ground pepper
juice of ½ lemon

Tzatziki
1 crisp cucumber, peeled and cut into 3-5mm
    (⅛-¼in) dice
1-2 garlic cloves, crushed
a dash of white wine vinegar or lemon juice
425ml (¾ pint) reduced-fat Greek yogurt or
    best quality natural yogurt
1 heaped tablespoon mint, freshly chopped
sugar, salt and freshly ground pepper

Mix the marinade ingredients. Cut the meat into 2.5cm (1in) cubes, season with salt and pepper and put into the marinade for 1 hour at least.

Put the cucumber dice into a sieve, sprinkle with salt and allow to drain for about 30 minutes. Dry the cucumber on kitchen paper, put into a bowl and mix with the garlic, vinegar or lemon juice and yogurt. Stir in the mint and taste. It may need seasoning with salt, pepper and a little sugar.

Drain the meat and thread onto metal skewers or kebab sticks. Grill for 7-10 minutes over a barbecue, turning and basting with the marinade two or three times, serve with a green salad and tzatziki.

Nutritional value per serving:
Calories: 235
Fats: 12g
Carbohydrates: 4g
Salt: 0.64g
Saturated fat: 6.2g
Fibre: 0.3g

SERVES 6-8 (MAKES 24)

PREPARATION TIME: 30 MINUTES

COOKING TIME: 10 MINUTES

trimmed lamb cutlets with salsa verde & olives

24 lamb cutlets

olive oil, for brushing

rosemary sprigs and lemon slices, to garnish
  (optional)

Salsa verde

1 garlic clove

5 anchovy fillets

1 teaspoon capers

bunch of mint, finely chopped

bunch of flat-leaf parsley, finely chopped

1 teaspoon Dijon mustard

1 tablespoon red wine vinegar

6 tablespoons olive oil

salt and freshly ground black pepper

Olives

200g (7oz) pitted olives

bunch of rosemary

juice of 1 lemon

a little olive oil

Nutritional value per cutlet:

Calories: 123

Fats: 9g

Carbohydrates: 0g

Salt: 0.73g

Saturated fat: 3g

Fibre: 0.3g

First make the salsa verde: finely chop together the garlic, anchovies and capers, place in a large bowl and mix together to a paste. Add the chopped mint and parsley, mustard and vinegar. Stir together and, as you stir, slowly add the olive oil. Once this is all mixed in, season and chill.

Slice the olives, put them in a bowl and mix in the rosemary, lemon juice, a touch of oil, and salt and pepper.

Place the chops on the barbecue and brush them with olive oil. Grill the chops for about 3 minutes on each side.

Remove and place on a large warmed dish with the bone facing outwards like a handle. Dress all the chops with the olives, followed by the salsa verde.

TIP

Generally, lamb chops are sold from the butchers in racks of about 6 cutlets. You can ask your butcher to cut them - you want your racks cut into cutlets with all the fat trimmed off. Alternatively, if you're going to cook a lot of cutlets, pre-order the number you'd like.

baked **potatoes** with dill & yogurt sauce

16 large 'old' potatoes

Dill and yogurt sauce
450ml (16fl oz) sour cream or fromage blanc
2 teaspoons Dijon or grainy mustard
225ml (8fl oz) natural yogurt
6 tablespoons fresh dill, chopped
$\frac{1}{2}$ teaspoon salt
sugar to taste

Scrub the potatoes well, prick them in 3 or 4 places with the tip of a knife. Wrap them in tin foil and bury in the hot coals of a barbecue for 45-60 minutes. Meanwhile mix all the ingredients together for the sauce. To serve, cut a cross in the top of each potato and spoon in some dill and yogurt sauce.

TIP

Of course these potatoes can equally be baked in a hot oven, but the flavour of potatoes cooked in coals is just so delicious that it is worth the bother.

Nutritional value per serving:
Calories: 202
Fats: 6g
Carbohydrates: 33g
Salt: 0.29g
Saturated fat: 3.6g
Fibre: 2.4g

black bean, corn & roasted red pepper salad

275g (10oz) dried black beans

1 garlic clove

dried chipolte chillies

1 large onion, halved

175g (6oz) long grain rice

1 tablespoon olive oil

225g (8oz) cooked corn (about 4 ears)

2 sweet red peppers, roasted, peeled, deseeded
   and diced

2 tablespoons fresh coriander or mint

2 tablespoons fresh parsley

6 spring onions, chopped

Dressing

50ml (2fl oz) red wine vinegar

2 tablespoons lemon juice, freshly squeezed

1 clove garlic, crushed

1½ teaspoons toasted and ground cumin seed

½ teaspoon toasted and ground coriander

175ml (6fl oz) olive oil

Nutritional value per serving:

Calories: 583

Fats: 31g

Carbohydrates: 64g

Salt: 0.07g

Saturated fat: 4.5g

Fibre: 6.1g

Soak the beans in cold water for at least 3 hours or overnight. Next day drain them and place in a large pot with the garlic, chillies and onion. Cover with fresh water and bring to the boil. Continue to simmer for 1-1½ hours or until the beans are tender.

Meanwhile, make the dressing by whisking all the ingredients together in a jar. When the beans are tender but still intact, remove the onion, garlic and chillies. Drain and toss in the dressing while still warm. While the beans are cooking, cook the rice also: bring a large pot of water to the boil, add salt and the rice and bring back to the boil for 5-10 minutes or until the rice is tender. Drain and toss in the olive oil. In a large bowl, mix the beans with the rice, corn, red peppers, coriander or mint, parsley and spring onions, and more dressing. Taste and correct seasoning if necessary.

How to roast and peel peppers

Preheat the oven to 250°C/475°F/gas mark 9. Put the peppers on a baking tray and bake for 20-30 minutes until they are soft and blistered. Place in a bowl and cover with clingfilm. Leave to cool. Peel the peppers and remove the seeds but do not wash them.

sala

sid

aubergine & coriander dip

1 large aubergine

1 garlic clove, crushed

$1/2$ teaspoon sea salt

$1/4$ teaspoon ground black pepper

$1/4$ teaspoon ground cumin

2 dessertspoons extra virgin olive oil

1 tablespoon chopped coriander

Preheat the oven to 190°C/375°F/gas mark 5.

Bake the aubergine whole with the stalk left on for 40 minutes, or until the skin has browned and it feels very soft to touch. Leave to cool, then peel.

Place all the other ingredients except the coriander in a liquidiser or food processor along with the aubergine flesh, and blend until smooth. Stir the coriander into the mixture and serve with flat bread.

Nutritional value per serving:

Calories: 117

Fats: 10g

Carbohydrates: 5g

Salt: 1.26g

Saturated fat: 1.3g

Fibre: 4.1g

devilled plums

450g (1lb) plums, stoned and diced

3-4 spring onions, chopped with their green

1 teaspoon honey

juice of 1 lime

1 red or green chilli, deseeded and
    finely chopped

Toss the diced plums with the spring onions, dress with honey and lime juice, and finish with a sprinkling of chopped chilli.

TIP

Serve this tart little relish with bean dishes.

Nutritional value per serving:

Calories: 44

Fats: 0g

Carbohydrates: 11g

Salt: 0.01g

Saturated fat: 0g

Fibre: 1.8g

SERVES 4

PREPARATION TIME: 10 MINUTES

COOKING TIME: 10 MINUTES

MARINATING TIME: 1 HOUR

date and **blood orange** salad

juice of 1 lime and 2 lemons

grated zest of $^1/_2$ lime and 1 lemon

$^3/_4$ teaspoon ground cinnamon

1 teaspoon orange flower water

2 tablespoons caster sugar

4 blood oranges, peeled and thickly sliced

12 fresh dates, halved, stoned and cut into strips

pinch of *ras-el-hanout* (see TIP)

Put the lime and lemon juice and zest in a bowl, add a pinch of the cinnamon, plus the orange flower water and sugar and mix well. Leave for 1 hour at room temperature. Place in a pan and boil for 5 minutes to form a light syrup. Remove from the heat and leave to cool, then chill.

Place the orange slices and dates in a bowl and pour over the chilled syrup. Sprinkle over the *ras-el-hanout*, sprinkle over the remaining cinnamon to taste, and serve.

TIP

Ras-el-hanout is a North African spice mix made up of some 30 different spices, including dried roses, cardamom, turmeric and cloves. Look for it in Middle Eastern shops and specialist food shops.

How to peel and slice citrus fruit

Cut the top and bottom off the fruit, then stand on one end and cut slices downwards to remove the peel and pith. Turn the fruit on to its side and cut into slices.

Nutritional value per serving:

Calories: 184

Fats: 0g

Carbohydrates: 45g

Salt: 0.04g

Saturated fat: 0g

Fibre: 4g

marinated grilled vegetables

Marinade

1 tablespoon extra-virgin olive oil

1 tablespoon balsamic vinegar

1 teaspoon honey

2 teaspoons lemon juice

salt and freshly ground black pepper

1 aubergine, sliced into 1cm ($\frac{1}{2}$in) rounds

1 red pepper, cut in half lengthways, cored and
   deseeded

1 red onion, sliced lengthways

2 courgettes, sliced lengthways 5mm
   ($\frac{1}{4}$in) thick

6 cherry tomatoes

4 asparagus spears, trimmed

small handful of oregano, chopped

small handful of basil, chopped

small handful of parsley, chopped

$\frac{1}{2}$ 400g (14oz) can kidney beans, drained
   and rinsed

Mix the marinade ingredients and reserve.

Place the vegetables under a high grill until they begin to blacken and are soft. The red pepper should be cooked skin-side up. Remove from the heat and allow to cool. Peel off the red pepper skin and cut into strips. Place the vegetables in a bowl. Add the herbs and beans to the bowl. Pour over the marinade and mix well. Leave to marinate for 1-2 hours.

TIP

Make double the quantity and serve this dish as a main course, accompanied by rice, couscous or polenta.

This dish is high in iron, fibre and folic acid, as well as Vitamins A, B6 and C.

Nutritional value per serving:

Calories: 240

Fats: 8g

Carbohydrates: 33g

Salt: 1.17g

Saturated fat: 0.9g

Fibre: 11.9g

wok-fried choi sum with shiitake and tamari

450g (1lb) choi sum (Chinese flowering cabbage)

2 tablespoons groundnut oil

1 garlic clove, crushed

1 tablespoon finely chopped fresh ginger

110g (4oz) shiitake mushrooms

75g (3oz) fresh or canned Chinese water chestnuts, peeled and thinly sliced

100ml (3$\frac{1}{2}$fl oz) chicken stock

2 tablespoons cornflour

2 tablespoons tamari (or dark soy sauce)

1 tablespoon sesame oil

1 tablespoon roasted peanuts

Separate the stems from the leaves of the choi sum and cut them into pieces 5cm (2in) long. Blanch the stems in boiling salted water until just tender, then drain well.

Heat a wok or deep frying pan, add the groundnut oil, garlic, ginger, choi sum stems, mushrooms and water chestnuts and stir-fry for 3-4 minutes. Add the choi sum leaves and cook for a minute longer.

Blend the stock with the cornflour to form a paste and stir it into the pan. Stir in the tamari and sesame oil and toss well together. The sauce should form a glaze around the vegetables. Sprinkle over the peanuts and serve immediately.

Nutritional value per serving:

Calories: 158

Fats: 10g

Carbohydrates: 13g

Salt: 2.13g

Saturated fat: 1.7g

Fibre: 0.2g

baked onion with carrot & cumin sauce

10 x 275g (10oz) round white onions

unscented vegetable oil

1.5 litres (2$\frac{1}{2}$ pints) vegetable stock

450g (1lb) bulgur (cracked wheat)

2 tablespoons olive oil

500g (1lb 2oz) corn kernels, cooked

200g (7oz) pine nuts

8 plum tomatoes, peeled, deseeded and diced

$\frac{1}{4}$ tea cup flat-leaf parsley, chopped

$\frac{1}{4}$ tea cup fresh mint, chopped

juice of 1 lime

salt and freshly ground black pepper

Carrot & Cumin Sauce

unscented vegetable oil

3 shallots, sliced

1$\frac{1}{2}$ teaspoons cumin seeds

700g (1lb 8oz) carrots, chopped

1 garlic clove, chopped

300ml ($\frac{1}{2}$ pint) white wine

1 litre (1$\frac{3}{4}$ pints) vegetable stock

Nutritional value per serving:

Calories: 423

Fats: 15g

Carbohydrates: 55g

Salt: 1.5g

Saturated fat: 2.2g

Fibre: 4.7g

Preheat the oven 180°C/350°F/gas 4. Line baking trays with non-stick paper. Remove the outer skins of the onions, leaving the root and stalk intact. Cut the top off the onion to create a lid. Scoop out the middle using a spoon or melon baller. Brush the insides with unscented vegetable oil and season. Place on the trays in the oven and bake for about 20-25 minutes. Remove and leave to cool. Pour the stock into a large saucepan and bring to the boil. Reduce the heat, then add the cracked wheat and simmer for about 15-20 minutes, or until all the stock is absorbed. Add the olive oil and stir. Add the corn kernels, pinenuts, tomatoes, herbs and lime juice; stir well and season. Fill the prepared onions with the mixture and replace the onion lids.

Heat a little unscented vegetable oil in a saucepan. Add the shallots, cumin, carrots and garlic; sauté for about 3-4 minutes. Pour in the white wine and reduce by half. Add the vegetable stock, bring to the boil and simmer for 20-25 minutes. Season, remove from the heat and allow to cool slightly. Blend until smooth and pass through a fine sieve.

Cover the onions loosely with foil and place in the oven for 8-10 minutes. When cooked, place an onion in the centre of each plate, pour on the sauce and serve.

TIP

If you can get hold of Vidalia onions for this recipe use them - they are so sweet and delicious.

button sprouts with parmesan & pearl onions

3 tablespoons olive oil

20 small pearl onions, blanched and peeled

1 tablespoon light muscovado sugar

40g (1½oz) unsalted butter

200ml (7fl oz) meat stock

350g (12oz) button sprouts (baby Brussels sprouts)

2 tablespoons freshly grated Parmesan cheese

salt and freshly ground black pepper

Heat the oil in a frying pan in which the onions will fit in a single layer, add the onions and cook over a high heat until golden all over. Add the sugar and half the butter and cook until the onions are caramelised, about 8-10 minutes. Pour in the stock and cook until it has evaporated.

Meanwhile, cook the Brussels sprouts in boiling salted water until just tender but still retaining a little bite. Drain them well.

In a separate pan, heat the remaining butter until foaming, add the sprouts and sauté for 5 minutes, until golden. Add the onions and toss together, then season with salt and pepper and transfer to a serving dish. Sprinkle with the Parmesan and toss to coat.

TIP

Brussels sprouts are a strange vegetable, inspiring either love or hate. Here are some great ways of serving them:

• Tossed with roasted chestnuts and celery

• Puréed and finish simply with nutmeg and butter

• Mixed with reduced-fat crème fraîche and seasoned with a little curry powder

Nutritional value per serving:

Calories: 242

Fats: 19g

Carbohydrates: 12g

Salt: 0.57g

Saturated fat: 7.5g

Fibre: 4.3g

carrots and **beetroot** with north african spices

12 very small beetroot

4 tablespoons olive oil

6 carrots, cut into slices 1cm (¹/₂in) thick

50g (2oz) unsalted butter

¹/₄ teaspoon ground coriander

¹/₄ teaspoon cumin seeds

¹/₄ teaspoon ground cinnamon

1 teaspoon lemon zest

1 teaspoon light muscovado sugar

pinch of saffron strands, soaked in 2
   tablespoons hot water for 10 minutes

1 teaspoon finely chopped coriander root (well
   washed), if available

1 tablespoon chopped fresh mint

salt and freshly ground black pepper

Preheat the oven to 190°C/375°F/gas mark 5. Wash and trim the beetroot, leaving 2.5cm (1in) of the top attached, but do not peel. Place in a shallow baking dish, pour over the oil, then cover with foil and bake until tender when pierced with a small knife, about 40-50 minutes. Uncover and leave to cool for 15 minutes, then peel them and cut in half vertically. Cook the carrots in boiling salted water until just tender, then drain and refresh under cold running water. Melt the butter in a large frying pan, add the spices, lemon zest, sugar and saffron and cook for 1 minute. Add the beetroot and carrots and the coriander root, if using, and toss together gently. Season to taste, transfer to a serving dish and sprinkle over the mint before serving.

How to zest lemons

Paring the zest of lemons or other citrus fruits is simple if you use a small tool called, believe it or not, a zester. This removes fine strands of peel but leaves the pith intact so it doesn't taste bitter.

Nutritional value per serving:

Calories: 270

Fats: 22g

Carbohydrates: 17g

Salt: 0.44g

Saturated fat: 8.1g

Fibre: 4.4g

red bean salad with artichokes

450g (1lb) cooked red kidney beans (canned
  is fine)

2 cardoon sticks or 6 artichoke hearts, sliced

lemon juice

1-2 fresh chorizos, sliced

2-3 tablespoons olive oil

1 red onion, finely sliced into half moons (see
  page 144)

1 tablespoon crumbled or chopped oregano

salt

Trim, scrape and slice the cardoon or artichokes. Cook in a little water for 10-15 minutes until the vegetables soften. Stir in the beans, reheat and leave to cool.

When you're ready to serve, fry the chorizo slices in the oil until caramelised and crisp - don't let them burn. Pour the contents of the frying pan onto the beans, salt lightly and finish with lemon juice, onion and oregano.

TIP

Pencas, the rosettes of a wild artichoke, a member of the thistle family and one of the first wild vegetables of spring in some parts of the world, can also be used in this recipe.

Nutritional value per serving:

Calories: 244

Fats: 11g

Carbohydrates: 25g

Salt: 1.88g

Saturated fat: 2.6g

Fibre: 8.4g

saffron-braised potatoes with paprika

4 tablespoons olive oil

700g (1lb 8oz) new potatoes, lightly scraped

3 garlic cloves, crushed

1 tablespoon tomato purée (or passata)

1 tablespoon coriander seeds

$1/2$ teaspoon hot Spanish paprika

good pinch of saffron strands

750ml ($1^1/4$ pints) well-flavoured boiling chicken stock

1 tablespoon chopped fresh coriander

salt

Heat the olive oil in a wide saucepan with a lid. Add the potatoes and sauté for 2-3 minutes without letting them colour. Add the garlic and cook for a minute longer, then stir in the tomato purée, coriander seeds, paprika and saffron. Add a little salt, then pour on the boiling stock, cover and simmer for 30 minutes, until the potatoes are tender. Raise the heat and boil until the liquid has reduced to a thick sauce, turning the potatoes occasionally. Sprinkle with the coriander and serve hot.

TIP

This dish can also be served cold as a first course or salad.

Nutritional value per serving:

Calories: 247

Fats: 12g

Carbohydrates: 31g

Salt: 0.94g

Saturated fat: 1.5g

Fibre: 2g

rice and **vegetable** timbale

1 large carrot, trimmed, peeled and grated

1 mouli (white radish), trimmed, peeled and
grated

$1/2$ celeriac, trimmed, peeled and grated

2 beetroots, trimmed, peeled and grated

400g (14oz) cooked basmati rice

2 tablespoons finely chopped flat-leaf parsley

1 tablespoon finely snipped chives

110g (4oz) raisins

2 tablespoons extra-virgin olive oil

8 whole chives

Mix the grated vegetables thoroughly with the cooked rice.

Add the parsley, snipped chives, raisins and olive oil and stir again.

Firmly press the mixture into timbale pots and refrigerate for at least 1 hour before turning out.

Decorate with the whole chives.

Nutritional value per serving:

Calories: 296

Fats: 7g

Carbohydrates: 56g

Salt: 0.26g

Saturated fat: 1.2g

Fibre: 4.4g

rice & lentils with crispy onions

700g (1¹/₂lb) onions (about 4 onions), finely
   sliced
125ml (4fl oz) olive oil
1 litre (1³/₄ pints) water
250g (9oz) brown lentils
250g (9oz) long-grain rice
salt and freshly ground pepper

Heat the oil in a sauté pan, add the onions, toss and cook until richly golden.

Bring the water to the boil, add the lentils and cook for 20 minutes. Add half the fried onions and the rice. Season with salt and pepper. Stir well. Cover and cook on a very low heat for about 20 minutes or until both rice and lentils are cooked. Taste and correct seasoning if necessary.

Meanwhile continue to cook the remaining onions in the sauté pan until crisp and caramelised. Serve the rice and lentils at room temperature decorated with the crispy onions.

How to cut onions into half moons
Cut the onion in half lengthwise. Peel each half and place cut-side down on the chopping board. Cut into fine half circles.

Nutritional value per serving:
Calories: 488
Fats: 20g
Carbohydrates: 66g
Salt: 0.28g
Saturated fat: 2.7g
Fibre: 5.3g

cassava with garlic and lime

1.3kg (3lb) cassava root, peeled and cut
   into chunks (see TIP)
4 tablespoons olive oil
4 cloves of garlic, crushed
4 tablespoons lemon or lime juice
salt

To finish
fresh coriander, chopped
cassava chips

Boil the cassava chunks in salted water for about 30 minutes until soft – don't worry if they disintegrate at the edges. Drain thoroughly.

Meanwhile, in a small frying pan, heat the oil and lightly fry the garlic to soften. Add the citrus juice and bubble up. Pour the dressing over the cassava chunks and finish with a dusting of chopped coriander. Serve with cassava chips.

TIP
Cassava can often be found in Caribbean markets and in some supermarkets - its brown hairy skin is often waxed to protect it and to increase its shelf life. Make cassava chips by slicing the root very finely on a mandolin and deep-frying or microwaving.

Nutritional value per serving:

Calories: 426

Fats: 11g

Carbohydrates: 84g

Salt: 0.28g

Saturated fat: 1.6g

Fibre: 3.8g

double-baked sweet potatoes

2 large sweet potatoes

1 teaspoon extra-virgin olive oil

1 small onion, finely chopped

$\frac{1}{2}$ teaspoon ground cumin

$\frac{1}{2}$ teaspoon ground coriander

4-5 button mushrooms, chopped

dash of soy sauce, to taste

1 teaspoon dried oregano

sesame seeds

Preheat the oven to 190°C/375°F/gas mark 5.

Bake the sweet potatoes whole for 40-50 minutes until soft.

Gently fry the onion for 5 minutes in the olive oil. Add the mushrooms and spices to the pan and fry for another 5 minutes. Add the oregano and soy sauce and remove from the heat.

Cut each sweet potato in half lengthways and gently scoop out the flesh, being careful not to tear the skin. Add the flesh to the onion mixture and mix together well, adding more soy sauce if you like.

Place the potato skins on a non-stick baking tray and fill with the onion mixture. Sprinkle with a few sesame seeds. Bake in the centre of the oven for 20 minutes then serve immediately.

TIP

This dish is high in Vitamins A, C and E, and is a good source of fibre.

Nutritional value per serving:

Calories: 213

Fats: 4g

Carbohydrates: 42g

Salt: 0.47g

Saturated fat: 0.7g

Fibre: 5.1g

sweet
treats

spiced baked apples

275g (10oz) sultanas

225ml (8fl oz) brandy

1 teaspoon ground cinnamon

$\frac{1}{2}$ teaspoon ground allspice

110g (4oz) light soft brown sugar

10 medium cooking apples (preferably Bramleys)

10 whole cloves

Place the sultanas in an airtight jar, pour in the brandy and store in a cool, dry place until required.

Preheat the oven to 160°C/325°F/gas mark 3.

Place the sultanas in a bowl, then add the cinnamon, allspice and sugar. Stir until combined. Core the apples, keeping them whole; do not peel them. Score the outsides around the middle. Place in an ovenproof dish, large enough that the apples will not touch – this allows them to cook evenly. Fill the apples halfway with the fruit mixture, place a clove in the centre of each one, then fill to the top with the remaining fruit. Pour about 125ml (4fl oz) cold water over the bottom of the dish, then bake the apples for about 45 minutes, or until they are soft and slightly puffed but still holding their shape.

Remove from the oven and leave to cool for about 5 minutes. Place each apple in a bowl and serve, pouring the syrup that collects at the bottom of the baking tray over the apples.

Nutritional value per serving:

Calories: 213

Fats: 0g

Carbohydrates: 42g

Salt: 0.03g

Saturated fat: 0.1g

Fibre: 2.2g

sweet potato purée

450g (1lb) sweet potato, peeled and sliced
350g (12oz) unrefined caster sugar
8 tablespoons water
1 orange, juice and zest
$1/2$ lemon, juice and zest
1 short stick cinnamon
1 tablespoon butter
2 eggs, separated
salt

To finish
cream
powdered cinnamon (optional)
few curls orange zest

Cook the potatoes until tender in enough lightly salted water to cover – they'll take about 40 minutes. Drain, allow to cool a little, and peel. Or bake in the oven and skin. Mash the flesh to a purée.

Meanwhile, melt the sugar in the water with the orange and lemon zest and juice and cinnamon, and bring to the boil. Simmer for 5 minutes and set aside. Remove the zest and cinnamon stick, and combine the hot syrup with the mashed sweet potato. Return the mixture to the heat and beat it with a wooden spoon until it thickens to a soft purée which holds its shape on the spoon.

Remove from the heat and beat in the butter. Allow to cool a little and beat in the egg yolks. Whisk the egg whites and fold them in. Allow to cool and pile into pretty glasses. Finish with a lick of cream, an optional sprinkle of powdered cinnamon and a few curls of orange zest.

TIP

This is often made with the white-fleshed sweet potato which, though less sweet than the orange-fleshed varieties, is considered to have a finer flavour. Either will do.

This pudding is a good source of Vitamins A, C and E.

Nutritional value per serving:
Calories: 351
Fats: 6g
Carbohydrates: 76g
Salt: 0.36g
Saturated fat: 3.1g
Fibre: 1.5g

pink grapefruit & pomegranate sorbet

1 litre (1³/₄ pint) pink grapefruit juice
    (about 10 grapefruit)
225g (8oz) caster sugar
1 egg white (optional)
1-2 pomegranates

Garnish
2 pink grapefruit cut into segments
pomegranate seeds
a little sugar
fresh mint leaves

Put the freshly squeezed grapefruit into a bowl, add the sugar and dissolve by stirring it into the juice. Taste. The juice should seem rather too sweet to drink: it will taste less sweet after freezing. Cut the pomegranates in half around the 'equator'. Open out and carefully flick the seeds into a bowl, discard the skin and all the yellow membrane.

Pour the mixture into the drum of an ice-cream maker or sorbetiere and freeze for 35-40 minutes. Fold in the pomegranate seeds. Scoop out and serve immediately or store in a covered bowl in the freezer until needed.

Before serving, chill the plates in a refrigerator or freezer. Then put 1-2 scoops of sorbet on chilled plate and garnish with a few segments of pink grapefruit. Sprinkle with pomegranate seeds, spoon a little grapefruit juice over the segments, decorate with fresh mint leaves and serve immediately.

TIP

For straight pink grapefruit sorbet, simply omit the pomegranate seeds.

Nutritional value per serving:

Calories: 355

Fats: 0g

Carbohydrates: 92g

Salt: 0.06g

Saturated fat: 0g

Fibre: 2.4g

coconut milk, yogurt and red chilli sorbet

1 small hot red chilli

500g (1lb 2oz) caster sugar

500ml (18fl oz) water

1 x 400ml (14fl oz) can of unsweetened
    coconut milk

250ml (8fl oz) plain yogurt

4 tablespoons white rum

Cut the chilli in half lengthways, remove the seeds and dice very finely. Place in a pan with the sugar and water, bring to the boil and simmer for 1-1$^{1}/_{2}$ minutes or until the sugar has completely dissolved. Remove from the heat and stir in the coconut milk, yogurt and rum. Leave to cool.

Pour into a sorbetière and freeze until firm, following the manufacturer's instructions. If you don't have a sorbetière, pour the mixture into a bowl and place in the freezer. After 30 minutes, when the mixture is beginning to set, remove it from the freezer and beat well with an electric beater or hand blender to disperse any ice crystals, then return it to the freezer. Repeat this two or three times, then leave until the sorbet is set firm.

TIP

In general, the smaller the chilli, the hotter it is. Always buy chillies that are firm to the touch. Once they become soft, they lose their fresh flavour.

Nutritional value per serving:

Calories: 659

Fats: 11g

Carbohydrates: 137g

Salt: 0.42g

Saturated fat: 9.3g

Fibre: 0g

rose petal sorbet with summer fruits

110g (4oz) rose petals

600ml (1 pint) water

200g (7oz) granulated sugar

zest and juice of 1 lemon

1 egg white (optional)

225g (8oz) summer fruits (strawberries, raspberries, blueberries, redcurrants, blackcurrants etc.)

Trim and discard the white part of the rose petals. Place the water and sugar in a pan and bring slowly to the boil ensuring the sugar has dissolved before boiling point is reached. Boil for 2 minutes then remove from the heat and add the rose petals, along with the lemon zest and juice. Stir well and leave to cool. Cover and chill overnight in the refrigerator.

The following day, pour the syrup through a sieve lined with a piece of damp muslin. Reserve 6 dessertspoons of the syrup and set aside. Transfer the remainder to the bowl of an ice-cream maker and churn until frozen. If using the egg white, whisk it to soft peaks and add to the sorbet when semi frozen. Continue churning until completely frozen. Spoon into a chilled freezerproof container and freeze until required. Prepare the fruits according to their type. Divide between six tall glasses, add a dessertspoon of rose syrup to each glass and top with scoops of the sorbet. Serve at once.

TIP

Choose rose petals with a really sweet scent and a vibrant colour. Deep pink or crimson give excellent results. The best time to pick them is when the flowers are wide open, just before they start to fade.

Nutritional value per serving:

Calories: 142

Fats: 0g

Carbohydrates: 37g

Salt: 0.02g

Saturated fat: g

Fibre: 0.8g

watermelon crush

125g (4^1/$_2$oz) caster sugar

250ml (9fl oz) water

1kg (2lb 4oz) watermelon flesh (a 2kg/4lb 8oz
   melon yields approximately 1kg/2lb 4oz flesh)

juice of 1 lemon

Combine the sugar and water in a small pan and heat gently to dissolve the sugar. Increase the heat and boil for 2 minutes. Remove from the heat and cool.

Cut the melon into wedges, remove and discard the skin. Roughly cube the flesh, prising out the pips as you go. The handle of a teaspoon is a useful gadget for this.

In a food processor or liquidiser mix the melon cubes with the sugar syrup and process to a smooth purée. Add lemon juice to taste.

Pour the mixture into an ice-cream maker or sorbetière and churn until frozen. If you don't have an ice-cream maker, pour the purée into a shallow container and freeze for 45 minutes to 1 hour. During this time ice crystals will start to form around the edges of the container. Remove the granita from the freezer and break up the crystals with a fork using a stirring and scraping action Return to the freezer and repeat every 45 minutes until you have a glistening mass of crystals. This can take 2-3 hours. Cover the container and freeze until required.

TIP

Serve within 1 to 2 days of making.

Nutritional value per serving:

Calories: 101

Fats: 0g

Carbohydrates: 25g

Salt: 0.01g

Saturated fat: 0g

Fibre: 0.1g

banana bread

450g (1lb) very ripe bananas (3 large ones), skinned

110g (4oz) honey

2 medium eggs

110g (4oz) butter, softened

110g (4oz) light brown sugar

225g (8oz) self-raising wholemeal flour

1 level teaspoon baking powder

1 teaspoon freshly grated nutmeg

To finish

1 banana, skinned and quartered lengthways

Preheat the oven to 180°C/350°F/gas mark 4. Butter and line a 23 x 15cm (9 x 6in) loaf tin with buttered greaseproof paper or butter paper.

Purée the bananas thoroughly with the honey and the eggs in the liquidiser or food processor. Beat the butter with the sugar until light and white, then beat in the banana mixture, alternating with the flour sifted with the baking powder and spice, and blend thoroughly. Drop the mixture in the loaf tin, spreading it well into the corners. Top with the finishing bananas.

Bake for an hour, until the cake is shrunk from the sides, well-risen and springy in the middle – it may need a little longer, in which case turn the oven down a notch and bake for another 10-15 minutes. Tip it out onto a baking rack to cool.

TIP

This bread is all the better for a few days in the tin so can be made well in advance.

Nutritional value per serving:

Calories: 487

Fats: 18g

Carbohydrates: 78g

Salt: 0.68g

Saturated fat: 10.3g

Fibre: 4.4g

banana & cashew slices

4 tablespoons sunflower oil

250g (9oz) bananas (approximately 2 medium
   bananas), skinned

$1/2$ teaspoon vanilla essence

1 teaspoon ground cinnamon

$1/4$ teaspoon ground cardamom

50g (2oz) cashew nuts

50g (2oz) dessicated coconut

50g (2oz) oats

1 apple, peeled and grated

Preheat the oven to 190°C/375°F/gas mark 5.

Blend the oil, bananas, vanilla essence, cinnamon and cardamom in a liquidiser or food processor. Add the cashew nuts and blend for a few seconds to break them up.

Add the coconut, oats and apple and blend for a few seconds more.

Turn into a greased 23cm (9in) baking tin. Bake in the centre of the oven for 25-30 minutes. Leave to cool, then cut into wedges.

Nutritional value per serving:

Calories: 185

Fats: 13g

Carbohydrates: 15g

Salt: 0.01g

Saturated fat: 4.5g

Fibre: 2.3g

carrot & dried fruit puddings

110g (4oz) dates, diced

110g (4oz) dried figs, diced

25g (1oz) stem ginger, diced

250ml (8fl oz) boiling water

40g (1½oz) raisins

½ teaspoon bicarbonate of soda

1 teaspoon baking powder

60g (2½oz) unsalted butter

60g (2½oz) caster sugar

2 free range eggs

175g (6oz) self-raising flour, sifted

200g (7oz) carrots, coarsely grated

½ teaspoon ground cinnamon

½ teaspoon ground mixed spice

Preheat the oven to 190°C/375°F/gas mark 5. Put the dates, figs and ginger in a bowl, then stir in the boiling water, raisins, bicarbonate of soda and baking powder. Leave to stand for 15 minutes.

Beat the butter and sugar together until pale, then beat in the eggs one at a time. Fold in the flour, then stir in the dried fruit mixture, grated carrots and spices. Pour the mixture into 6 timbales or ramekins, 200ml (7fl oz) in capacity, or into an 18cm (7in) ovenproof dish. Place on a baking tray and bake for 30-35 minutes for individual puddings or 40-45 minutes for one large one, until they are risen and golden and a knife inserted in the centre comes out clean. Leave for 5 minutes before turning out.

Serve with double cream or fresh vanilla custard and a compote of dried fruits.

Nutritional value per serving:

Calories: 371

Fats: 12g

Carbohydrates: 64g

Salt: 0.94g

Saturated fat: 6.4g

Fibre: 3.8g

mixed berry corn **muffins**

250g (9oz) rice flour

170 g (6oz) polenta

1½ teaspoons bicarbonate of soda

2 tablespoons soft brown sugar

250g (9oz) fresh or frozen mixed berries, such
as cranberries, blueberries, blackberries,
redcurrants or blackcurrants

1 dessert apple, cored, peeled and grated

170g (6oz) yogurt

2 tablespoons lemon juice

1 tablespoon sunflower oil

150ml (¼ pint) unsweetened apple juice

Preheat the oven to 200°C/400°F/gas mark 6.

Sift the rice flour, polenta and bicarbonate of soda into a bowl. Add the sugar, berries
and apple, and mix well.

Mix the yogurt, lemon juice, oil and apple juice in a jug, pour into the bowl and stir in
to make a soft batter. You may need a little extra apple juice. It should easily spoon into
a non-stick fairy cake tin, putting 1 spoonful into each case. You should have enough for
10-15 muffins.

Bake in the centre of the oven for 15 minutes, or until golden. Leave to cool, then
transfer to a wire rack.

TIP

These muffins freeze well. Make them well in advance then defrost and serve with warm
with custard or crème fraîche.

Nutritional value per serving:

Calories: 188

Fats: 2g

Carbohydrates: 41g

Salt: 0.56g

Saturated fat: 0.4g

Fibre: 1.7g

index